HOW TO GET CHASED BY THE PRESS WITHOUT HIRING A PR FIRM

CAMERON HEROLD
ADRIAN SALAMUNOVIC

FREE PR

How to Get Chased by the Press without Hiring a PR Firm

ISBN 978-1-61961-528-1 *Hardcover*

978-1-61961-530-4 *Ebook*

FROM CAMERON:

To my two boys, Aidan and Connor—you've been in my heart and mind every day of this journey.

FROM ADRIAN:

To my amazing mother, Marie-Claire, who gave me the confidence, skills, and education to make this all possible.

CONTENTS

FOREWORD

Back in 2006, I was sitting on a flight, listening to the person next to me explain what he did for a living. He was a scientist who did something that involved feeding cocaine to rats, and then measuring some chemical in their brains. I'm not joking. The guy got free 100 percent pure cocaine from a government lab and fed it to rats. Kind of makes your job sitting behind a desk look pretty boring, huh?

But I digress. We exchanged cards, and that was that. A few weeks later, I got a phone call from a friend of mine who was a reporter at a major daily newspaper. She was doing a story on addiction and called me because she believed I knew everyone. (I have massive ADHD. I do, in fact, talk to everyone.

It's one of the best parts of ADHD.) I told her about my encounter with cocaine-rat guy and put the two of them in touch.

Two weeks later, this scientist with whom I'd spend probably an hour and a half with en route from Newark to Chicago was now featured in a huge article on the front page of a major newspaper. Let's just say that his next round of grant funding came to him *a lot* easier.

That interaction and the subsequent media result was one of the first times I ever thought about creating something like Help a Reporter Out (HARO), which is now the world's leading connection tool between journalists and sources. Less than four years after my in-flight encounter with cocaine-rat guy, my idea was acquired by a company called Vocus (now Cision), and my life radically shifted for the better.

See, that's what PR can do. It can take you from no one to someone overnight. It can save your business. It can make you a hero or make you a million dollars. It can bring you fame and fortune, and it can even elevate your position from "just another scientist" to "one of the world's leading scientists specializing in how the brain handles addiction."

See where I'm going with this?

Prior to HARO, it cost a *lot* of money to get PR. People didn't have access to journalists or even understand who was covering which beat. Reporters change jobs every five minutes. Who knows what anyone is working on at any given time, especially since most journalists are working on eight things at the same time. Before HARO, you sucked it up, hired a high-priced PR firm, paid them your first born, and hoped for the best. That's how it was, for years and years and years.

HARO changed that. It democratized how PR is achieved, and it launched a whole new way of getting your brand in front of an audience.

Still, though, it's kind of tricky. You need the rules, the guidelines, and the tips and tricks to make it happen. Do it without those, and your success will be muted, at best.

That's where Cameron and Adrian come in.

They've written the ultimate guidebook for those looking to get press, grow their brand, and get in front of the masses. *Free PR* is the roadmap you've been looking for. It's the definitive guide to walk you through the process of getting the media's attention, no matter what your company does. It's mandatory reading for anyone looking to do their own PR in a world where the concept of "doing your own PR" doesn't exist.

I should know. I helped create the concept.

Enjoy the book. You're going to get a ton out of it.

—PETER SHANKMAN
Founder, Help a Reporter Out
@petershankman
www.shankman.com

INTRODUCTION

Common lore tells us that getting media attention is a complex, almost scientific process that involves hiring public relations firms or consultants who have magical inroads the rest of us don't have access to. In the interest of our business, we pay an average of $5,000 or more per month to these PR magicians, who may or may not deliver on what they're selling.

Still, we pay, because what other options do we have?

The answer is: we have plenty of other options. Not only are these options effective, but they're also *free.*

Perhaps you've heard of 1-800-GOT-JUNK?, a

junk-removal service. Its former chief operating officer and this book's coauthor, Cameron Herold, will be the first to admit that junk removal is not necessarily the most glamorous or sexy service. Nonetheless, Cameron managed to grow the business from $2 million to $106 million in revenue and from fourteen head office employees to 3,300 system-wide employees in just six years.

Cameron accomplished this spectacular growth almost solely through media placement—in other words, through PR. In just a few years' time, Cameron built out the internal PR team and systems that landed 1-800-GOT-JUNK? more than 5,200 individual media stories. Among those were huge media hits like *Fortune, Wall Street Journal, New York Times,* CNBC's *Squawk Box*, and the holy grail, the *Oprah Winfrey Show.*

Perhaps you've noticed that Cameron's title at the company had nothing to do with public relations. He didn't need any specific degrees or training. There weren't any consultants or external PR firms involved. He built a small internal team, and he used little more than the cost of his own time. He opened these doors for himself through creativity, research, dedication, and his own vision.

While Cameron went on to teach CEOs at major international companies how to grow and scale their businesses through the same strategies he employed at 1-800-GOT-JUNK?, coauthor Adrian Salamunovic was busy working his own magic out of a 600-square-foot apartment in Ottawa. With no more funding than his credit card, Adrian launched DNA11—a company that specializes in turning images of DNA into art. He had no advertising or PR budget to spend and nothing to lose.

Adrian personally reached out to *WIRED*, *Playboy*, and Discovery Channel, as well as a handful of influential blogs. All of them ran with the story. To put this in context, at the time, it would have cost $50,000 to run an advertisement in *WIRED*. Instead, Adrian earned more meaningful editorial space in the same publication for no cost at all other than being interesting. As a result, DNA11 garnered press coverage that generated more than $80,000 worth of holiday sales in just one month. Throughout its first year, DNA11 continued to use PR as its only form of advertising—the *best* type of advertising, because it was free and reputable. It worked. In its first year, DNA11 raked in more than $1 million in sales.

Despite the fact that he was now running a profitable company, Adrian continued to utilize this exact same strategy to fuel DNA11's businesses for many years to come, ultimately generating tens of millions of dollars in revenue. He then used the same process and methodologies we will cover in this book to scale CanvasPop, an e-commerce photo-printing company, to eight figures in revenue, mostly using the power of free PR. The fact is, almost *any* business can benefit from PR and apply the strategies outlined in this book, no matter what industry you're in.

On his own accord, Adrian scored hits at highly visible media outlets such as *The Big Idea with Donny Deutsch*, and even an entire plotline on an episode of *CSI: NY* at the point when it was one of the most-watched television shows worldwide. Adrian has experienced few more thrilling moments in life than watching that episode of *CSI* with his family and friends in the very same apartment where he launched DNA11 just a few years before.

Over the years, Adrian has gone on to score exposure for his companies and others in sought-after media outlets, such as the *New York Times, Wall Street Journal, The Verge,* Mashable, *Today Show*, and hundreds more. In the course of this, he learned that with the right process in place, there are no limits to where a company can appear for free.

THE CURRENT PR MODEL IS BROKEN

Perhaps you're wondering, "Well, if it's so easy to get press for my business, then why am I paying all of this money to a PR agency every month?" The answer is: you shouldn't be. The current public relations model is broken.

Think about it like this: you're spending the equivalent of a full-time salary on a consultant who is likely only focused on you for one day a week. The hard work—the critical work—of developing story angles that will capture the attention of a reporter is assigned to this public relations rep, who you have to hope will craft quality story ideas. If they fail, which there's a strong possibility they will, then you've lost out on a significant amount of money with nothing to show for it.

Part of the problem is that the PR rep you hire will only have a superficial understanding of your company culture, lore, and the ins and outs of your business. They aren't passionate or dedicated to telling the world about your company because they care; they're acting solely out of financial interest. There's nothing wrong with this—after all, that's business. But is this model serving you right? Probably not.

Perhaps you, like so many other companies, signed on with a PR firm because you were sold on the company's list of contacts and relationships with the press. After a while, you come to find out that either (1) those media relationships aren't as solid as initially claimed, or (2) the PR firm only solicits their high-level media contacts on behalf of bigger, more established companies than yours.

So you start to wonder, "What am I paying this PR firm for, anyway?" Good question. In fact, we hope you're asking yourself that question. If you're not, you should be, because there is a better way for you to attain your PR goals minus the frustration, disappointment, and cost of hiring a PR firm.

The answer: do it yourself. For free.

When Cameron joined 1-800-GOT-JUNK? as COO in October 2000, the company was paying a San Diego-based PR firm $5,000 per month to generate media hits. Cameron had a term for this strategy: "a waste of money." Instead, he reached for his phone and, within two weeks, landed more press than the expensive PR firm had generated in the past six months. 1-800-GOT-JUNK? fired their PR agency and hired their first in-house person to do the job. Every single month from thereon out, that in-house person outperformed the PR agency five times over.

YOU CAN DO IT TOO

No matter what you may have been told (or, more accurately, *sold*) to the contrary, the two of us are not doing anything you can't do yourself. In these coming pages, we'll show you how we've achieved massive PR hits over and over again without spending money on agencies. We'll share our exact strategy. The tools you'll employ are simple, affordable, and effective. Providing you have a strong product or service and are willing to put in the time and effort PR takes, this strategy will work for you just like it has worked for us.

The tools in this book will work for any type of business. Whether you have a business-to-consumer model or a business-to-business model, whether you're selling a product or a service, the principles remain the same. These tools also work across all sectors, including retail, e-commerce, SaaS companies, apps, and anything in-between. The strategies we'll employ are equally effective for all media outlets, including television, print, online publications, radio, podcasts, and even trade journals.

We'll walk you through how to find the right media outlets; target the right journalists to pitch your stories to; develop the essential stories that your in-house PR team will pitch again and again for maximum results; prepare for interviews with television, radio, print, and online reporters; and demonstrate how to build a dynamic in-house PR team.

REMEMBER YOUR PR PURPOSE

Just in case you're wondering, "Is PR *really* important enough to go to all this trouble?"—the answer is *yes*. It absolutely is.

A public relations strategy that is well executed will

accomplish five primary purposes that are critical to the success of your business. PR is the gift that keeps on giving.

BRAND AWARENESS

If no one knows about your company, do you exist? Well, yes—but you're probably not very profitable. Public relations allows you to create brand awareness. People need to know you're there in order to bring their business to you. Once they are aware of and have tested your brand, they begin to trust you and to build a relationship with your company.

TRAFFIC AND ORGANIC REFERRALS

When people are aware of your presence (and when you offer a desirable product or service), they will come to you. Media links generally result in traffic and organic referrals for years to come. You can capitalize on this attention with sign-ups, subscriptions, and sales. Traffic ultimately allows you to spread your message, cultivate customers, and, most importantly, drive actual revenue while reducing customer acquisition costs (CAC) compared to relying on just paid advertising.

LINK JUICE

When an online publication links back to you, it creates not only traffic, but also search engine optimization (SEO). The more traffic you receive, and the more links from credible media sources you have, the more Google understands that your company is important, and the higher up you go in search results.

SOCIAL PROOF

At the end of the day, we're all monkeys. Monkey see, monkey do. If everyone sees that media and influencers are acknowledging your company, it serves as social proof or credibility. Since the people and media sources that matter most are talking about you, other people will, too. There's no better way to create instant credibility with prospective clients and partners.

If you'd like some quick evidence of social proof, Google either of our names or our company names, and you'll see the impact our lessons will have for you, too.

RIPPLE EFFECTS

An interesting thing happens when one or two journalists write about you: *more* journalists write about you. The more journalists who write about you, the more people want to partner with you. Public relations creates a cycle, which makes your life easier and easier. Remember this as you begin to pitch to journalists: your first pitches will be the most difficult, as you begin the task of stirring up interest. Eventually, the ripple effect kicks in, and not only are more media outlets interested in your pitches, but, eventually, they'll start coming to you.

NINETY-NINE NOS

The strategies in this book *will* work; however, it's important to go into this understanding that doesn't mean all of your story pitches will be accepted. In fact, the vast majority of them won't. It's the same for every major company and PR agency out there. What matters, though, is that you get those few yeses that matter—and that you leverage each and every yes you get.

PR is all about hustle and perseverance. You will get a lot of nos. But all it takes is one yes to change the destiny of your company. Both of us have experienced that life-changing yes. It happens. But it won't happen if you don't put yourself out there in a strategic and meaningful way. We're going to show you how to do exactly that.

THINK BIG TO WIN BIG

If you're a CEO, it's important that you get involved in your company's PR efforts, because well-executed PR has the power to advance your vision, strategy, and goals for the organization. (And if you're not a CEO, it's up to you to make your CEO aware of the role they need to play in your PR efforts.) This includes increasing sales, strengthening your brand, appealing to top talent, and any other goals and aspirations you might have.

CEOs will want to understand the ins and outs of PR because they'll likely play an important role in identifying the target audience and crafting story angles that can't be ignored. Not to mention the fact that they will likely often be the face of the company once your PR team lands stories.

With this strategy in place, you'll be able to generate

PR either by yourself or in-house, depending upon your business's size and budget. Your company will score major media hits that *make* you money without *costing* you money in the process.

The most important thing to remember is this: the biggest limitation to effective PR is often you. You have to believe in your story. Think big, and know that anything is possible if you set your mind to it.

WORKING WITH THE MODERN MEDIA

CHAPTER ONE

UNDERSTANDING THE MEDIA CLIMATE TODAY

Today's media is quite different from the media we knew a decade ago. The climate has changed. The good news is it has changed to your benefit. Once you understand these changes and how they impact the way in which journalists (or reporters—we'll use these words interchangeably) select and write stories, you'll begin to see why free PR works.

First and foremost, understand that media is a business, not a public service. When print media was alive and thriving, its advertising revenue was much higher. More advertising dollars meant that more revenue was available for reporters and investigative journalism. Back then, journalists were more likely to hunt down their own stories, do research, craft angles, and present the results to the public.

Today, not so much. Lower margins mean there are fewer reporters. Coupled with the prominence of digital media and the need to constantly churn out new content as quickly as possible, these already short-staffed journalists are on shorter deadlines.

Because of that, reporters are looking for stories that arrive gift-wrapped and hand-delivered. This is the function of public relations in a nutshell—presenting reporters with stories and angles that can be easily crafted into a journalistic piece.

Even at this, PR professionals might have you believe that getting those stories into the hands of a reporter requires a seasoned specialist with a list of contacts. Not true. With a little bit of research, this information is readily available.

Pull back the curtain, and you will see that just as there is no wizard, neither is there an impenetrable wall of separation between journalists and you. That's right—there's no need for a middle man. All of this put together means you can generate your own press.

A WORLD'S WORTH OF MEDIA OPPORTUNITIES

When Cameron decided to bring 1-800-GOT-JUNK?'s PR program in-house, he hired someone with zero experience in the PR field, taught him the five angles (more on this in chapter three) the company wanted pitched to the media, and set him loose. Despite the fact that this employee didn't have any preexisting media contacts, he landed seven stories in a month. After about a year, Cameron hired two more employees. Once again, people with no specific PR experience began generating about seven stories per month in no time at all.

Perhaps you're wondering how this sort of success rate is possible for a novice. Easy. We pitched every story angle city by city. If the *Chicago Tribune* covered a story about us, then we would pitch the exact same story to the *Boston Globe*, the *Dallas Morning News*, the *San Francisco Chronicle*, and so on. These widespread media outlets began running the same story, which was fine because we were dealing with different reporters and separate audiences.

It was through this that Cameron came to realize what he had suspected: the media simply needs good content. If you approach reporters in the right way, they will tell your story and call it news.

Let's also not forget that, along with the reach and diversification that hitting local media outlets provides, there are also more media outlets than ever before. In addition to digital forms of traditional media, influencers and content providers are reaching huge audiences by leveraging disruptive, newer channels like YouTube, Twitter, and Instagram. This is an incredible development for free PR because these outlets constantly need new stories and ideas to keep our social feeds filled with fresh content.

THE BUSINESS OF MEDIA

Before we get too far ahead of ourselves, let's establish how the business of media works. At its core, media is a mouthpiece for the people and companies behind the stories it tells. Yes, it provides important information to the public, but in this day and age, it tends to serve more as a source of entertainment than a real watchdog for society. While it's true that some hard-hitting, investigative journalism does still exist, it tends to be limited to specific publications, such as the *New York Times* and *Washington Post*. Even these outlets include noninvestigative content as well.

Everyone has a story to tell. And that story is told to the media primarily through pitches and press releases distributed via email. Media outlets and individual reporters are swamped with hundreds of these emails a day. (We'll discuss how to stand out amid this inbox slam in the coming chapters.)

Not as glamorous as you may have envisioned, right? Gone is the romantic age when wily reporters uncovered corruption, when hard-drinking editors stood up to their greedy advertisers, and when journalists did lots of digging to unearth novel products for consumers.

But we're not writing this book for you as a consumer. We're writing it for you as a PR department.

Rather than bemoan the necessary financial and content changes that the media has undergone (which is a subject for a book of its own), consider instead what this means for you as you employ the media to tell your story.

WHERE YOU FIT IN

Don't forget that this process is a quid pro quo. You're providing a valuable service to the media, just as the media is providing a valuable service to you. Media outlets constantly need raw, fresh content, which they can polish, shine, and package as a product to sell to the consumer. What they offer is no different than laundry detergent or bread. You have something they need to sell their product, and they have something you need to sell yours. This is the circle of life in the media world.

You're doing a reporter a favor by providing material to help them do their job. You're putting that person's mind at ease that there will be something to fill a content void.

Think back to your high school English class. Remember the creative writing assignments? The teacher would stand in front of the class and say, "Today, you're going to write a story about anything you want. You have thirty minutes. Go!"

Did you feel your nervous system start to jangle just reading that? This is the tyranny of the blank page. When you can write about literally anything, how do you even begin to decide where to start? If you're like most of us, you would probably spend at least fifteen minutes of the next half hour banging your pen against the desk, wondering what to write about amid an infinite number of topics.

Reporters face this prospect every day. They're constantly on the hunt for a story. Our job is to help provide them with inspiration. That is PR. It is not hucksterism, charlatanism, or chicanery of any kind. It's simply providing a new thread to the tapestry of shared information that we consume as a product called "news."

The media needs the content these journalists provide, because it's how they sell advertising. The price that customers pay to digest media in whatever form doesn't even come close to reflecting the actual costs necessary to produce the product.

Advertisers or sponsors pay the substantial additional costs to gain exposure to a built-in audience.

In a very real sense, what the media outlet is selling is you, the customer. The days when circulation subscription fees could cover the costs of reporting, producing, and selling content are gone. Now it's all about the advertising dollars. Companies pay for the opportunity to be in the same space where you are, so they can pitch their products or services to you.

Since advertising is how a media outlet's bread is buttered, it will attempt to sell more advertising at higher rates. But they need a strong product that attracts readers or viewers. This is where strong, quality content comes into play.

And this is where you slide in.

By wrapping up your story for the media to tell, everyone wins. You get your message delivered, reporters get fresh content, the consumer gets an entertaining or informative story, and the advertisers get to hawk their wares before a large audience.

All of this means that content producers are more

eager than ever before to hear your ideas. It's hard to find new things to cover, so really you're helping by pitching them your stories.

THE ATTENTION ECONOMY

To understand media today, we also have to understand culture and technology. The changes in media over the past decade or so are directly related to shifts in these two areas. Because the world has changed, so has the way in which people digest media.

It's no mistake that some of today's most successful businesses are Facebook, Instagram, and Netflix. The reason these companies are worth a lot of money is because the most valuable asset a company can have is attention. These three companies garner a lot of attention. Attention, in turn, drives free exposure that leads to advertising and revenue. Therefore, attention directly translates into power.

There is no clearer example of the sheer power of attention today than President Donald Trump. Plain and simple, Trump won the election because he was able to draw so much attention to himself.

Even the negative attention ultimately contributed to his victory.

Now, we're certainly not making the argument that your company's road to success should include stirring up negative publicity. It shouldn't. However, Trump's presidency nonetheless exemplifies the power of attention, which is important to understand for our purposes.

Another clear example of success in the attention economy is Kim Kardashian. Love her or hate her, the fact remains that she is a master at grabbing attention. That attention translates to big dollars. Everything Kardashian touches turns to gold, from video games to makeup lines to clothing and fitness products. She has captured the attention of both the media and the public; because of that, she has also captured the market.

The other important thing to understand is that, because attention is such a valuable commodity, there are also more people vying for consumers' attention than ever before. Once upon a time, advertising was more or less limited to three main television networks and a local paper. Today, advertising is super-targeted and everywhere we look. We are surrounded by noise—thousands of tweets on our timelines, dozens of messages in our inbox, too many YouTube channels to count, and the list goes on. Everything is multiplied exponentially. Because there are so many different mediums through which companies are attempting to get their audience's attention, it makes it all the easier for audiences to tune them out. After a while, it gets to be too much. However, this doesn't mean that getting your audience's attention is impossible. Not at all. It's just that it is critical to get your audience's attention in the *right* way.

This explosion of outlets to feed the attention economy also means there is more opportunity out there than ever before. Once upon a time, there was a bottleneck effect, since only a handful of major media outlets decided what should be covered. Today, there are more places to pitch than ever before if you're willing to put in the work.

From a PR standpoint, attention translates to visitors and traffic. Attention plays a big role in creating your brand, and it's through branding that you create trust and repeat customers. These then lead us back to wealth and power. You can see how this is all very cyclical.

It is for this reason that the media is so important to your business. Media can draw attention your way, which is invaluable. There are some particular types of media that are especially valuable.

TYPES OF MEDIA

Now that you understand why you are important to the media, it's also important to understand how and why the media is important to you. There is, of course, the obvious reason that media offers you exposure. However, you could obtain this exposure through a variety of other methods as well, such as advertising and social media. So, with those avenues available to you, why take the time to roll out a PR strategy to land media hits as opposed to some of your alternative options? Let's take a look.

Today, there are three primary types of media that every business can utilize to draw attention to their products and services—some to greater effect than others.

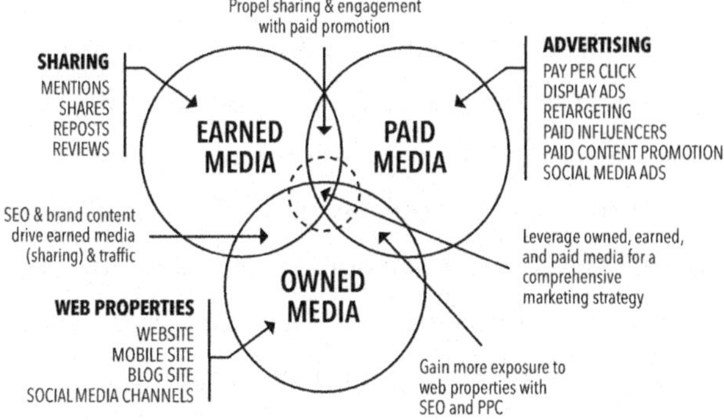

PAID MEDIA

Paid media is basically another word for advertising. In this day and age, paid media can refer to anything from billboards to commercials to banners to pay-per-click ads on social media sites. The primary issue with this form of media is abundantly obvious—it's expensive. Not only that, but 80 percent of the time, your message will be ignored despite the amount of money you're churning out to get it to the masses. Ironically, paid media is also ever more expensive and competitive.

One of the biggest problems with paid media is that consumers are savvier and more educated than ever before. They know an advertisement when they see it, even if it's in the guise of something else. Consumers value authenticity and, to most, advertisements don't fall under that umbrella. Also, from a practical standpoint, disruptive advertising, such as pop-ups and television commercials, gets in the way of the media people are actually trying to consume. I think we can all agree that's just annoying. Annoying is definitely not the impression you're looking to make on potential customers.

There's a saying that goes, "Advertising is like sex. If you have to pay for it, you're a loser." Obviously, this isn't always true, but it is funny—and there's an important kernel of truth in there. If, as a small or growing midsize business, you find that your only alternative is paid media, it's a red flag that your company is not that interesting or, more accurately, that you haven't figured out a way to convey your story in a way that's interesting.

When you turn to paid media, you are basically forcing the market. You have to force attention to your business by way of paying for advertising, or no one will take notice.

Of course, there are caveats here. As companies

scale and grow, they often can't rely solely on the press writing about them, so they have to run ads. For example, Coca-Cola is a great company, and they still have to pay for media. In this case, it doesn't mean they're doing anything wrong, it's just an issue of scalability. They have to run ads to stay top-of-mind.

OWNED MEDIA

Owned media refers to channels under your jurisdiction or that are owned by you. This includes your website and social media channels. Because you own these channels, you get to determine their messaging. You can change your messaging, you can test different strategies, and you can basically say or do whatever you want to.

Owned media is great for messaging; however, since it's not disruptive, there's no way to guarantee that the people you're trying to reach will find you. The greatest marketing strategy ever on an owned channel is worth nothing if the audience you're trying to reach never sees it.

What owned media *is* great for is spreading your

earned media hits even further. We'll discuss how to create engagement around your earned media hits later in this book.

EARNED MEDIA

Earned media is where we want to focus our PR efforts, and it is the form of media we'll concentrate on from here on out. Earned media refers to articles or stories online and in print media publications, influencer channels, television, radio, and podcasts. It is aptly named because we have to *earn* this form of media exposure. Another name for earned media is word-of-mouth.

Whereas paid advertising is often disruptive, earned media is engaging. Consumers are making the *choice* to digest the information that comes through earned media channels. They are drawn in either by content, context, or value.

Some companies are incredibly adept at earned media—Airbnb, TOMS Shoes, and Charity Water all come to mind. Each of these companies is constantly getting media attention for the things they do. And, of course, Virgin Group founder, Richard

Branson, is the king of earned media. He's constantly in the news, pulling some kind of crazy stunt. Because of this, everyone between the ages of fifteen and sixty knows exactly who Branson is and, by extension, what Virgin is. This is not an accident. Everyone knows who Richard Branson is precisely for the reason that he's the master of manipulating media attention. And, to be clear, that's not a bad thing.

Branson is a celebrity because he's made himself a visible figure. However, you don't need to be a celebrity to make earned media work for you. In fact, another masterful example of an excellent use of earned media is someone whose name I'm sure you *don't* know, despite the fact that you may very well know his story. His name is Kyle MacDonald.

MacDonald—perhaps better known as "the Paperclip Guy" or through his website, RedPaperclip.com—is a blogger who bartered his way from a red paperclip all the way up to a house.

In just a year, MacDonald transformed that paperclip into a home by making one trade up after another online. He went from a paperclip to a camp stove to a Kiss snow globe to an afternoon with Alice Cooper to a house. MacDonald was able to accomplish all of these upgrades because he drew attention to himself and his project. He garnered a ton of media attention from huge outlets, such as BBC, CBC, MTV, the *New York Times*, the *Wall Street Journal*, the *Today Show, Good Morning America*, and the list goes on. MacDonald didn't pay for a lick of advertising for his venture. His story earned him media.

NEXT STEPS

Now that you understand the lay of the land, you can probably see why the convergence of several factors has changed the PR game. Yes, you need the media—but the media also needs you. Still, maybe you still don't believe you have what it takes to get the job done. We can assure you, you do. In the next chapter, you'll find out why.

CHAPTER TWO

HOW THE MEDIA GETS STORIES

We've now established that there exists a symbiotic relationship between you or your PR rep and the media. You need them, and they need you. You can get exposure for your business, and the media company gets attention and traffic, which directly translates into money. The reporter looks good for generating quality content, and the outlet you've targeted improves.

WORKING WITH JOURNALISTS

Even knowing all of this, there still exists a certain mystique around journalists. We've been conditioned to believe that we can't just shoot off an email or phone call to them. It's true enough that doing either of these things without a plan in mind probably won't net the best results. However, there is no reason you can't reach out to journalists directly. Plenty of people do. And those same people who reach out to journalists are generally the ones who are making the news.

Perhaps you're still intimidated. We promise you that once you reach out and contact working journalists, you will quickly realize they're like you—simple human beings trying to do their job and earn a living. The only difference is their job is to create new content.

Think of the reporter like a pretty girl in high school who nobody asks to the prom because everyone assumes she'll turn them down. Chances are, she would have said yes to anyone who bothered to ask her out. Similarly, most journalists would love to hear from you, providing your story is something their audience will be interested in.

Journalists are constantly on the lookout for their next story, and they want new ideas and fresh voices. This is great news for you! It means they welcome your well-crafted story pitch. In a very real way, you're doing the journalist a favor by giving them an idea and lead for the content they need to create.

Like any other relationship, the best relationships with journalists are cultivated by viewing them as a two-way street. If you see a journalist as no more than a device to bring attention to your company, you're probably not going to see great results. It's much more effective to look at it like this: you work for the journalists, and your job is to make *their* job easier by handing them the story in a way that's both compelling and easy to understand. This includes packaging your pitch in such a way that the journalist can easily pass it along to their audience without a lot of heavy lifting.

THE BIG MYTH

As you consider the changing news industry, think about Spiderman. The superhero's alter ego, Peter Parker, is a newspaper reporter. His editor is constantly yelling at him to go find the story, so he grabs his camera and hurries out of the building. That is what the industry used to look like. Today, when he's yelled at to get a story, Parker will sit at his desk and sort through his emails to unearth an interesting pitch. Chances are, this winning pitch came from someone like you.

This antiquated idea of reporters running out of the office to hit the ground and dig up stories is what we call The Big Myth. Editors no longer smoke cigars in the office or stock their desk drawers with bourbon, and reporters don't wear fedoras or operate like shady private investigators.

What does this mean for you? It's simple: they want to hear from you.

EVERGREEN STORIES

The men and women bringing consumers the news are usually charged with bringing several stories to their morning editorial meeting. The more ideas they have to pitch to their editors, the better their chances of winning a spot in the day's news cycle and impressing the decision makers. Editors often come to the table with ideas as well, then dole these seeds out for stories to both in-house and freelance reporters.

Those who work in media understand that breaking news doesn't happen every morning. They're constantly on the lookout for what are called "evergreen" pieces. These are stories that are not time sensitive, but that can be stored up in the hopper, ready to go at a moment's notice. These are the stories that are usually called upon when a media outlet needs to fill space in its publication on slower news days.

Creating a fresh news feed is a necessary but difficult task. Sometimes stories come in shorter than expected, a sponsor pulls an ad, or a story is killed, for any number of reasons. The same is true in broadcast media, but in that case, the void is empty air.

No one understands better than reporters the fact that today's news cycle operates on a 24/7 basis. People no longer digest their news during set times like over their morning coffee or during their commute to work. Today, consumers also expect fresh news to digest when we look at our phones while waiting in line at the bank, while we're grabbing coffee on the go, as we scroll through our phones before going to bed at night, and even—let's be honest—when we're using the restroom.

Evergreen pieces are the media's contingency plan so that fresh news is waiting for consumers on all of these occasions that occur throughout the day. Look no further than *TechCrunch* for an example. On average, they publish upward of twenty stories a day; that's more than seven thousand stories per year! That also means there are seven thousand opportunities to get your story in front of their audience. Many media outlets publish many more stories than this every day—for example, *HuffPost* and *Buzzfeed*. Media outlets of all stripes are hungry machines, and they need to hear from you.

SEASONAL PIECES

In addition to evergreen stories, reporters also need seasonal pieces. These stories are intended to correspond with a specific time of year. Media outlets of all varieties create editorial calendars to determine when pieces will perform best and provide consumers with timely information. So, a story about turkey farming, for example, will likely run just before Thanksgiving. A story about grilling techniques will probably run sometime around Memorial Day or Father's Day.

The editorial calendar allows media outlets to plan ahead. It also provides a sense of how much new content must be gathered to complete a story. This sense of seasonality is something to keep in mind when pitching angles to the media. If you can explain how your story ties in nicely with the holidays, spring cleaning, or back-to-school, you'll have a better chance of convincing the media outlet to run your piece. This is one of the tricks of the trade that PR firms understand.

PRO TIP: FINDING THE RIGHT PR SKILL SETS FOR YOUR IN-HOUSE TEAM

In our experience, the most successful in-house PR personalities have a background in sales as opposed to marketing, writing, and *especially* public relations. You're looking for the person who loves to cold-call people, ask questions, and listen to answers—someone who is articulate and can convey their energy and enthusiasm across all mediums. This person should love your company, its culture, and core values, and be excited about where you're headed. It's also important that your PR person is viewed as the heart of the company, both internally and externally. Just another employee or drone won't cut it in this position.

You want someone who can handle rejection. They have to be comfortable hearing the word no all day long, without accepting it as a final answer. They require enough stamina to avoid burning out during the grind.

You also want someone who is tech savvy. PR success requires a lot of online research, apps, and using tools like a CRM. The more media savvy a person is in terms of understanding both what journalists and audiences want and how to package that message accordingly, the more successful your in-house PR program will be. Often, this ability is innate to those in sales.

Your PR person should be a competent writer with a proper command of grammar and spelling, sentence structure, vocabulary, and other fundamentals. Be aware, this doesn't mean you want to hire a writer or journalist by trade, because they often lack the sales skills necessary to thrive in this position.

Most important, as counterintuitive as it may sound, you are not looking for someone with a background in PR. A trained PR specialist will bring with them a lot of bad habits. They're used to spending all day writing press releases, wasting time talking to editors, and constantly dreaming up new angles to pitch. This is exactly what you don't want. It's what you're trying to get away from.

In other words, you're looking for someone with natural *hustle.*

PITCHES FROM PR REPS VERSUS FROM YOU

So far, none of this is too difficult to understand, right? What we want you to wrap your head around is that the PR firms you've been working with aren't doing rocket science. They just have a better understanding of the logistical elements we've discussed in this chapter so far. As soon as you grasp these basic concepts and what exactly it is that PR reps are doing, you'll be able to easily apply this knowledge and these skills to your own practice.

A PR company is, by definition, a middle man. As such, your PR representative's allegiance is, first and foremost, to the PR company—not you. The PR person is something of a mercenary as opposed to a local militiaman. That does not mean your hired PR rep won't do a great job on your behalf, but it *is* something you need to be aware of.

PR firms work on a retainer, which typically lasts for a three-month, six-month, or one-year term. Usually, the first month or two are designated as research time. The firm will gain an understanding of your company, craft story ideas, put together pitch steps and their plan for reaching out to the media, and share that plan with you, their client.

Anywhere from very little to no press is generated during this period. That's right—you will see nothing for your money for at least four to eight weeks.

This is important to note because a full-time employee charged with these same tasks will likely get all of this work done in a few weeks. Then it's off to the pitching races. This is one of the many benefits of having a PR person who is embedded in your company, living with your product or service, and in the loop with your culture. Chances are, even the best PR firm will never have the opportunity to know you or your product this intimately and innately.

After those first couple of months, the PR firm will assign someone to your account who will pitch stories to news outlets about once a week. PR firms generally explain this by saying they need to spend more time creating angles than pitching reporters. If you opt to put your press release out on the news wires (which we'll discuss in chapter five) so that they are available to reporters on a consistent basis, PR firms will charge an additional fee. This is something you can do internally at a much cheaper cost.

It is important to remember that your PR firm also

represents several other clients. This is the equivalent of dating someone exclusively, despite the fact that they are dating four or five other people. Who does that person really love? How much love are you getting from them? It will never be enough, because that person is being spread too thin.

You want someone who is exclusively in love with your brand and your culture—someone who's obsessed with it, who can pitch you and your company with the utmost sincerity. That sincerity is conveyed when they communicate with reporters in a way that's qualitatively different than a PR person does. As humans, we can read authenticity. We know when a person is truly passionate about something or someone. They exhibit more energy, enthusiasm, and excitement in a way that's palpable.

Even if you end up pitching the exact same story a PR firm does, there is still a marked difference in your favor. You are actually living and breathing the story every day. You are spending your time with the team who has created that story, and all of you are vibrating with the same buzz. That energy transfers and is absorbed. It can't be faked.

Journalists pick up on this, and it can make all the difference between inspiring a reporter to choose your story over someone else's. Journalists have a particularly strong and well-honed sense of authenticity, and they can differentiate between passion and routine performance. It's for this same reason that journalists love hearing from founders and CEOs. It's unlikely that anyone is going to have more passion or knowledge about a topic than the person who gave birth to it.

RELATIONSHIPS

PR firms claim to offer you access to the media. A PR rep's currency is that they've cultivated relationships with journalists who will provide coverage for their clients. And sometimes they do have access. But often they don't—at least no more than you do.

Even if a PR rep knows some reporters, there's no way they know enough to land you six or seven stories month after month after month. Journalists have loads of contacts who constantly pitch them stories. The idea that they only publish pitches from a single PR rep is absurd—not to mention, mathematically impossible.

Also remember that your PR firm is pitching their other clients to these journalists, too. It becomes a zero-sum game: your PR firm has to choose which client to pitch to a journalist who's looking for a single story. Now, had *you* gotten on the phone and passionately pitched to that journalist directly, it's entirely possible they would have chosen your story, rather than the several pitched by the PR firm.

There is another big reason to be wary of a third party working on your behalf, which you may have already realized based on our conversation thus far: transparency. If you're doing PR in-house, you can see what's happening at every single stage of the game. You can determine what's being done correctly, and what isn't. You can directly target the outlets you want and focus your efforts on any market you desire. Everything is under your control.

When you rely on an outside contractor to handle your PR, many elements of the process are inherently outside of your control. You have to trust that everything is being done well and is aboveboard. Remember, the PR firm wants to keep your business. Sugarcoating a situation, up-selling its services, and stringing you along might all be part of this at some point.

Lastly, if you do your own PR, you will own these media contacts and be able to easily reach out to them directly over and over again (providing you have a relevant pitch or story angle). Over time, you will likely get to the point where you have the mobile numbers of several high-profile journalists and have developed your relationship to the point where you can text them pitches on occasion. That is powerful.

Recently, colleges have begun offering public relations as a major. The skills students learn will allow them to get a job in a PR firm, but will their education teach them how to land six new stories per month? Probably not. While there is certainly value in learning the profession in a classroom setting, practical experience is often more helpful for many of the skills a successful PR person must cultivate.

A PR professor from a local university once visited 1-800-GOT-JUNK? to observe our methods. She was surprised by what she saw. In fact, after observing us for a while, she said we understood

PR on a deeper level than most. She realized we weren't doing things by the book. We weren't writing a press release, pushing it out on the wire with our fingers crossed, making some phone calls, and continuing to craft one story after another.

This is what you're "supposed" to do. But what we did actually got results.

One of the best PR people Cameron ever hired was a former writer for a small newspaper who happened to be a natural at sales. Her time as a writer allowed her to converse with journalists in their own language, and she was empathetic to their needs and desires. She understood the nature of deadlines, and when to approach a journalist. Many skills gleaned from other non-PR positions translate to great success in PR work. It's not about a set path, but, rather, a set of skills.

It's likely we could teach someone more about PR on the job over the course of a year than they would learn were they to study PR in college or at an apprenticeship in a PR firm. The mystique PR firms create around themselves isn't all that mysterious—and it's certainly not worth the steep price tag. At one company after another, we have taught people with no PR experience who have gone on to land seventy or more stories a year. Like many things in life, PR is best learned by doing.

NEXT STEPS

Generating your own PR will allow you to shape the message you truly want, target any market you desire, and monitor your results with absolute transparency. Next up, we'll start to take a look at how it all comes together.

CRAFT YOUR STRATEGY

CHAPTER THREE

KNOW YOUR AUDIENCE TO KNOW YOUR STORY

The first step of identifying the right journalists to approach and the correct story to pitch is gaining a specific and detailed understanding of your audience. You need to know who your audience is and what media sources they consume.

APPLY WHAT YOU KNOW ABOUT YOUR AUDIENCE

Chances are, you have already done market research on your audience from a sales perspective. You know who you're selling to, why you're selling to them, and how your product positively impacts their lives.

This information serves as the foundation to build your PR strategy upon as well. You want to use the information you already know about your target market to figure out which media sources they're visiting. With this, you'll likely simultaneously identify the media outlets that care about providing your target audience with information.

Let's say you've created a new jacket that is targeted to outdoorsy people. Start by thinking about your own social circle. Who do you know that fits into this archetype? Identify those people and have a conversation with them. Ask them what blogs they frequent, what podcasts they subscribe to, and what publications they follow on social media. This will give you a great starting point.

You may be surprised to learn that publications in the same space—that is, publications that cover the same topic—are different. For example, let's take a look at some of the leading publications that cover business. That category would include the *Wall Street Journal*, *USA Today*, *New York Times, Forbes,*

Fortune, Entrepreneur, Success, TechCrunch, and many others. However, while each of these outlets covers the broad topic of business, they all come at it from different perspectives and have a slightly different type of readership.

The *Wall Street Journal* is all about data, finance, and growth. They want to ask tough questions and get specific information about the facts, numbers, and data of your business. *TechCrunch*, on the other hand, is all about the scoop. They want to know all about VCs, founders, new products, and so on. *Forbes* and *Inc.* are very reader centric. They don't care about what you're launching. They care about *how* you did it and how it can help your readers. They deal in tips, rather than news. Somewhat similarly, the business podcast *How I Built This* wants founder stories. They want to know how entrepreneurs slayed the dragon, and what they learned along the way. You can see how all of these publications will draw upon specific niches of readers under the more general umbrella of business.

Then there's the fact that each media outlet includes subsections that focus on different topics. The *Wall Street Journal*, for instance, has a marketplace section, another section that covers sales and marketing, and another that focuses on finance.

All of this means that you need to research and learn about the specifics, not only of each publication, but also of each subsection of the publications you will potentially approach. This is how you will be able to narrow in on precisely the place your target audience is most likely to go to source their news.

For example, if I want to reach entrepreneurs, my PR campaign shouldn't target *USA Today*, because that's not their primary audience. Instead, I should solicit journalists at *Success*, *Entrepreneur*, *Inc.*, *Forbes*, and *Fortune*. These are the publications that my target audience tends to read.

Similarly, I don't want to try to pitch a story about oil and gas industry marketing strategies to *Success, Entrepreneur*, or *Fortune*. Their readers don't care about that content. They want to read in-depth profiles from Silicon Valley, news about what's happening with venture capital, and the latest innovative start-ups. Since these magazines are looking for those types of stories, that means the journalists who publish content on behalf of that magazine are looking for pitches on those topics.

Once you gain an understanding of the media sources your potential clients are investing their time in, that's where you want to generate press. It's here where you'll receive the most visibility to the people that matter, even if that means going to a smaller publication. It doesn't matter if you land an article in the *New York Times* if the vast majority of their readers don't care about the product you're selling. You're much better off going to a secondary media source whose audience is invested in your specific sector.

Cameron once had a friend—we'll call him Joe—approach him about getting a line in to land an interview on best-selling author Tim Ferriss's blog. Cameron replied, "But you don't even read his blog or listen to his podcast." When Cameron pushed Joe about which of Tim's blog posts most inspired him and served as a model for what he wanted to discuss, Joe stopped talking about getting in front of Tim's audience. That was the last Cameron heard from Joe on the matter.

Joe just wanted a big-time thought leader to talk

about him. This is a mistake many people make. Likewise, many of the company founders Adrian advises want to get into *TechCrunch.* There's no doubt that *TechCrunch* is a great outlet if you're trying to reach hardcore technology founders and the venture capitalist community. But that's not the audience most of these founders are looking to reach—they *are* that audience, which is why they're so focused on *TechCrunch.* This is an easy—and common—mistake. Just because *you* love a certain media outlet doesn't mean your target audience will, too.

Some people are unwilling to do the necessary groundwork to learn about the people who consume media from the sources they want to approach. Understand that this is an imperative you cannot skip. Without it, you can't know that you're crafting the right story or approaching the right journalists.

By the time you get to the point where you are communicating with a journalist, you want to be sure you have a story pitch that will sell itself. It's helpful to think about pitching a story as you would selling a product. If you were selling a product or service to a customer, you'd think about your customer's needs and how they will use your product or service. Then you would build that product to address the specifications of the customers' demands. Pitching a story is much the same. You want to build it to the specifications of the person who will use it. In this case, the person who will read, watch, or listen to it.

All we're talking about here is Business 101—discover what your prospect is interested in, then provide it. If you can't tell the journalist why their audience will care about your story, then you're not ready to pitch.

CREATING A STORY ANGLE

A story angle is the spin you are putting on your product or service that makes it interesting or compelling. It's what makes people care about your story. The angle has to be interesting enough both for the audience to want to consume it and for journalists to want to publish it. For example, it's not enough to go to a journalist and say, "I want you to write a story about an app I'm pushing live next week." That angle only serves you. It's just promotion. You want to encase this event in a context that's meaningful to others. For example, you want to explain how the app will make readers' lives easier or tie it to a current conundrum that a subset of people is experiencing.

However, one angle is not enough. You want to use different angles and stories for different media outlets. In doing this, it's crucial to put yourself in the shoes of a particular media outlet's audience. You have to intimately understand what that audience cares about. You have to understand precisely what interests them so much that they're inspired to invest their time and attention (and, perhaps, money) into reading an article, listening to a podcast, or watching a television program.

Over time, you will figure out the process that works best for you. Generally, we pitch a story angle to several journalists over the course of one or two months, then move on to another angle. Also, we often have more than one angle going at a time so that we can cater to a variety of journalists and outlet interests and readerships.

KNOW YOUR ANGLE

A good story angle that will grab both a journalist's

and audience's attention will make you stand out, is timely, and offers new or interesting information. That information will specifically appeal to a certain audience. In short, a good angle answers the questions: So what? Who cares? Why you?

Getting your story angle right is the single most important element of capturing media interest.

BRAINSTORMING ANGLES AND STORY IDEAS

There are four types of story angles. As you're brainstorming the angle that will work for you, the most important thing to keep in mind is your intended audience. Will this appeal to them? Is it compelling? Is it worth their attention?

The angle you choose for your story provides a perspective. It lays down parameters. Essentially, a story angle is the figurative version of a literal mathematical angle. For example, a ninety-degree angle is perpendicular at the point where the floor meets the wall. A 180-degree angle, on the other hand, is as if you just knocked down that wall. Everything above the floor is within the parameters of that angle. It's much more open-ended, rather than narrowly constrained. Likewise, a story angle puts limits on the scope of your pitch. It defines the shape of your story and provides context for the information you are providing. Your angle may be narrow or it may be open—either one can work. What's important here is that you understand the scope of your story and convey that scope accurately to the journalist when the time comes to pitch.

Once you understand how the media uses angles for its stories, you will begin to see them everywhere. You'll start to digest the media with two sets of eyes—one set focused on the content of the material, the other on the context. In other words, you'll begin thinking about *what* is being communicated while simultaneously considering *why*.

The angle you create will serve as the raw material a journalist will package into its finalized form, whether that's an article, blog post, video, podcast, or any other piece of content. Think back to that idea of creating a product for journalists. Your angle is the equivalent of a salesperson focusing on a handful of products, rather than an entire catalog. This limited scope allows you to have and provide intimate knowledge of each product rather than a superficial understanding of many.

Before you can create an effective angle, you must have a deep understanding of what makes your company unique or innovative in your industry. This is your Unique Value Proposition (UVP). What differentiates you from everyone else in a way that your audience will care about or be compelled by? This is an important part of framing your article.

CREATE YOUR UNIQUE VALUE PROPOSITION

Need help articulating your company's UVP? Visit freeprbook.com/tools for tips and tools.

THE FOUR STORY CATEGORIES

Generally speaking, there are four categories in which business stories can fit. Use these to begin to establish the parameter of your story angle and to trigger inspiration.

Announcements

Announcements are effective because they are

inherently newsworthy and novel. When Apple announces a new product, for example, the whole world listens.

We may not all be Apple, but announcements can still be newsworthy. It might be a new product, a new partnership, or a new hire. Announcements make a great dangling carrot because you are the only person who has that story, which means you can offer journalists an exclusive scoop on a new turn of events. For smaller companies, announcements generally work best in local or industry publications. As you build up a reputation and get more press, publications that have written about you in the past will also be interested in your announcements.

Evergreen

As we discussed in the previous chapter, media outlets love having evergreen stories on hand. They're also a wonderful category for you because you can get creative. Any company can come up with an evergreen story angle. Not only that, but these evergreen pitches can be pulled out and pitched all the time, at any time of the year.

Some great examples of evergreen stories are "how I did it," showing off your office or company; sharing the story behind the story; or even something offbeat like weird CEO rituals. These stories are fun and a great way of sharing your company's culture or narrative.

Seasonal

On the opposite end of the spectrum, we have seasonal stories. These are directly tied to specific events or holidays, such as back-to-school, the new year, or the beginning of spring. You can even get creative and tie them to the type of obscure national holidays that everyone loves to hashtag about on social media. Also, you can create a day that doesn't exist. If Dog Day doesn't exist and you sell pet food, guess what? All the better. You can designate a dog day.

One of the great benefits to seasonal stories is you can recycle them on an annual basis. For example, CanvasPop loves making an announcement every April 1 because we can get silly, and perhaps even weave in a bit of guerilla marketing (which we'll talk more about later).

START YOUR OWN HOLIDAY

Want to learn how to submit your own official calendar holiday? Visit freeprbook.com/tools.

Stunts and Events

The best thing about stunts and events is that they are potentially completely under your control. They also don't have to cost a lot of money. (We'll cover these in depth in chapter nine.)

Or, you can hitch your wagon to an event that is bigger than just your company. Say, for example, you are going to SXSW or CES (The International Consumer Electronics Show), so you want to capitalize on the media's presence and make an announcement. You'll have to make sure to stand out among the noise by making sure your announcement is something really new or interesting to that audience.

Announcements	Evergreen	Seasonal	Stunts and Events
Awards Funding Major hires Major partnerships Milestones New products	Company culture Contribute articles Customer success "How I did it" Infographics Office tours Product Reviews	Create your own day Major holidays Seasonal stories	Big stunts Celebrity and product placements Crazy products Pop-ups Trade shows Your own award or certification

THE FIVE STORY ANGLES

Within these four categories, you can narrow in on one of the five core story angles or archetypes. These will work for just about every business and sector. While you are not limited to these five story angles, they provide an excellent framework and will be particularly helpful as you begin rolling out your in-house PR program.

Overcoming Adversity

This angle provides inspiration and backstory. It reassures readers that there is a light at the end of the tunnel in their own struggles. It recounts the obstacles that your company has negotiated, and how your leadership kept the team together through hard times. It implies that it's all smooth sailing moving forward, and that the rough waters your company has traversed are a thing of the past.

A possible subset of this story angle is the origin story, which recalls how and why it all began. This angle is great for publications that like "how I did it" stories, like *Inc.* and *Success.*

The Culture

The culture angle describes the unique aspects of your company that set it apart from your competitors. It ties your company to the community in which it resides and demonstrates your value to that community.

Culture stories are great for outlets like *Fast Company, The Muse*, and anywhere else that likes to fuse culture and business.

Customer Endorsement

This angle allows you to demonstrate how your product or service benefits customers and helps them overcome problems or achieve success. It's also creates synergy, particularly in cases in which you can point to an example of a happy customer who is a respected entity.

This angle is a bit different than the others because a credible publication may very well ask to speak directly with one of your customers. In other words, if you are a start-up that is still establishing its base, this angle might be logistically tricky to pull off. Also, if you want to keep information about your customers close to the vest for the sake of confidentiality or to ward off potential competitors, one of the other four angles might be a better fit.

This angle can generally be pitched to a publication of any variety, providing you position it in such a way that it directly appeals to that outlet's audience.

Leveraging Technology

This type of story demonstrates how your company has employed technology to grow or become more efficient compared to your competitors. Companies that are good at adopting modern technology project a forward-thinking image.

This angle is ideal for technology-focused publications and websites, such as *TechCrunch* and TrendHunter.com.

The Future

This paints an inspirational picture of where your company is headed. It might include your Vivid Vision and Big Hairy Audacious Goal. Here, again, you can incorporate your origin story to draw a timeline demonstrating where your company began, where it is today, and where it will be tomorrow.

WIRED and other speculative magazines like *Fast Company* are a great match for stories of this variety. You want to find a publication that is focused on where things are going as opposed to where they are or have been.

CREATING YOUR STORY ANGLE

As you brainstorm your story angle, keep in mind that you are not writing the actual story, but, rather, packaging it so that the journalist can put their stamp on it and shape it into a final product. Your job is to provide the bullet points, the highlights, and the key issues. Your job is to provide the bones of the story. The journalist will apply the meat. Within this, however, there is still room for creativity, as long as you continue to keep your audience and the purpose of your pitch in mind. Think of it as writing the headline for the journalist in a way that will appeal to their audience.

Earlier, we mentioned that Adrian's company, DNA11, was featured on an episode arc of *CSI: NY.* As a fan of the show, Adrian understood that the product could be of interest to both the *CSI* audience and its writers. So, he took a chance and wrote a physical letter addressed to the producer, Anthony Zuiker, offering him a free DNA portrait as a gift. In doing this, Adrian brought the product to Zuiker's attention as a way of leveraging technology. Ultimately, Zuiker created an entire episode centered around the company.

MAKE YOUR ANGLE RELEVANT

In addition to considering your audience, you also want to take the present climate into account. What topics are currently trending that you might be able to build off of to better appeal both to your audience and to journalists?

We are big fans of trend analysis tools, such as BuzzSumo, Google Trends, and SEMRush. These analytics tools provide information about keywords and search volume so that you can see how many people are searching for specific terms at any given point in time.

Another example is if you're launching an iPhone app and taking advantage of a new sexy feature that Apple just added (for example, when they added Augmented Reality). Announcing that your app has something that uses that feature will exponentially increase your chances of getting coverage around the launch of the new iOS.

Relevance will draw more traffic not only to your business, but also to the media channel you publish on. Journalists appreciate this, and your odds of successfully pitching your article increase significantly.

REFINING ANGLES FOR DIFFERENT MEDIA SOURCES

Also remember that this isn't a one-and-done endeavor. Your goal isn't to have one phenomenal story. Instead, it's to have several good ones that will work in tandem to generate momentum for your company. The more you obsess about the perfect story, the less likely you are to realize it.

Your best strategy is to focus on one angle at a time, with a variety of different key points. You can then pitch this single angle any number of ways based on publication and readership, which creates a variety of potential stories. If your company raised a round of fundraising, you might make an announcement and mention the product within it. You can pitch this same story under the Future angle, by focusing on what this fundraising will facilitate and how that will draw you into the future, and under Overcoming Adversity, by explaining the hurdles you had to navigate to get to this point. Every source you pitch should have one leading angle, but that angle will often vary from one pitch to the next.

Each of these angles will likely be used multiple times. Your PR person can pitch these angles to multiple media sources and markets. Considering the number of media outlets in each market, you can get a lot of mileage from those five simple angles.

A single story angle can be rerun in different publications throughout the country on a variety of media platforms. Remember that the journalist is doing the actual writing, so the same angle will end up being a different story in each separate media outlet. You can get the same story about your company's culture to run in several different cities, or you can have it run in the top fifty business magazines. Or perhaps you might decide to get it covered by the top fifty bloggers or on the top fifty podcasts.

Let's say you come up with an Overcoming Adversity story angle. This single story angle is covered in fifty different local outlets and business publications. Assuming you have seen an uptick in sales or attention, you have now confirmed that your audience is, in fact, frequenting these media outlets. With this knowledge, you can now grab your Leveraging Technology story angle, and approach those same newspapers but target a different journalist writing for a different section. *Bam!* You've just grabbed fifty more media hits. But you're not done yet. Next, you can take your Customer Endorsement angle, and pitch it to the same publication, but, again, to different journalists who write for different sections. You get the point. With just five angles to pitch, you can easily generate at least two years' worth of PR.

PRO TIP: GROW YOUR PR DEPARTMENT

Begin your in-house PR department with one person. Once you have them slotted in the position, you will steep them in the company culture, its product, and services, and the history of the company. (If you have started off with an internal hire, this may not be necessary, or it might be necessary to a much smaller degree than with an external hire.) Together, you will work to shape the five first angles, which they'll pitch over the course of the next twelve months.

Next, this person will meet with the sales team and the marketing team to find out what those departments are focusing on over the course of the next year. How can PR outreach add to the sales and marketing efforts to help meet their goals? From there, your PR person will start to build out a list of targeted outlets to focus on throughout the duration of the year.

As you build out your PR team from one to two, three, or even four people over the course of the following few years, you want them to be situated very closely to the CEO and marketing and sales teams. The PR team needs to vibrate with the same energy, enthusiasm, focus, and mentality as those departments. If they're sitting in with operations, IT, or finance, they likely won't be privy to the right energy and passion for the tasks at hand. They need to know why their work is critical and how it's going to advance the company in some positive way.

Download a job description template for this role for free at www.freePRbook.com/tools.

HOW ANGLES HELP EXECUTE YOUR STRATEGY

Cameron has a client in Toronto who is trying to build a company culture that establishes his business as a top employer. He wants potential talent to view the company as one of the most desirable technology companies to work for in Toronto. With this goal in mind, regardless of the press outlet or story angle, he always injects a company culture angle into his pitch because he knows the more he talks about the company's culture, the easier it will be to recruit top talent.

This is an example of a company that is effectively using PR to advance and execute its strategy. Just as you use other divisions in your company to help you identify which publications to target, you'll also want to lean on them to help you craft the PR angles that will support the company's midrange strategy. Think about what your company wants to accomplish in the next two or three years, and embed this within your angle. In other words, start with your goals.

To do this effectively, you'll want to focus on questions like the following:

- Where is the company going?
- How will you accomplish your goals?
- What should you focus your attention on?

Once you have a clear understanding of the goals and direction of your company, you can craft story angles that support these initiatives. With that knowledge, you can now select the appropriate angle from the selection of angles you've created to achieve that goal. Let's say your company's goal is to promote growth. Ask yourself:

- Which of your possible stories would be most helpful in recruiting more employees?
- Which of the possible stories will establish your company as a great place to work or will attract senior-level talent?
- What story will help you retain more employees?
- What story will land you more national accounts?

With this, you'll also want to think about the story angle you're planning on pitching from the perspective of the audience. If you're stumped on how to do this, this is a good opportunity to mine one of your greatest resources: existing and prospective customers. This time, you'll want to gather data about the type of stories they read, their interests, and other details that will help you fine-tune your angle.

For example, you may learn that your customers are interested in supporting socially conscious brands. Armed with that knowledge, you can refine your angle to focus on how your company is doing volunteer work in the surrounding community, or you can talk about its charitable activities and partnerships. Both will appeal to your target customers and will position your company in the best possible light to the people you most want to connect with.

There is no journalist on your "beat" covering the ins and outs of what your company does. Nobody is going to shadow you for a week and a half or dig into what you're doing. In all likelihood, journalists probably don't care what you're doing. It's your job to present the journalist with a compelling story idea that paints the image you want to project while making their job easier in the process. And you do this by speaking directly to the journalist's audience.

NEXT STEPS

Now that you know your audience, your next step is to find the journalist who has the eyes, ears, and attention of that audience. Public relations specialists know the secret formula for doing this—and we're about to share it with you.

CHAPTER FOUR

COMPILING YOUR MEDIA LIST

As you begin your public relations efforts, you'll need to spend time identifying the journalists who cover your beat and target your audience in the media outlets your customers are frequenting. Over time, though, media outreach will become easier and easier.

While you always want to be aware of new media outlets and be building new relationships, you will also compile a catalog of media outlets and contact information. There will come a point when you can act almost immediately on a story angle because you'll know exactly which journalist to pitch it to right off the bat.

For now, though, you will want to be thorough in your research so that you can rest easy your pitch is landing in precisely the right inbox. While doing this initial research will require some time and diligence on your part, know that the public relations firms you're hiring are compiling their lists in much the same way. Just remember all of the effort you're saving with a little bit of elbow grease!

SOURCING ANSWERS

The last thing you want to do is randomly select media outlets to pitch. Strategy is key when it comes to PR. Your public relations efforts should be designed to move your company in the exact same direction as your sales and marketing efforts do (yet another reason why in-house public relations makes more sense and is more effective). When you align your sales and marketing strategy with your public relations strategy, you end up targeting the same clients in multiple ways. This results in an even bigger and better impression on the people you most want to connect with.

Begin by finding answers to these questions:

- What trade journals do your customers read?
- What outlets will give you the greatest direct benefits?
- What outlets will give you maximum exposure for your products/services/culture?

You don't have to—and shouldn't—do this work in a bubble. Talk to people in sales and marketing. Talk to your founder and CEO (although, you need to make sure their media slant is aligned with that of your target customers). Talk to people in *all* corners of your company, for that matter.

Once again, you should also feel free to mine that huge resource of yours: customers and prospective customers. Take the guesswork out of it, and learn about the media sources they love straight from the source.

If you have the opportunity to talk to customers face-to-face or over the phone, bring it up in conversation. You can also send out a survey. SurveyMonkey, Google Forms, and our favorite, Typeform, all allow you to create simple surveys to send out to customers, asking them about the media outlets they read or follow. You'll want to use Google Forms if you're polling a small group of twenty or so. Survey Monkey is great for larger groups because you can cross-tabulate, rather than creating a lot of individual answers.

You'll want to make sure your survey includes both open-ended and multiple-choice questions. Use the open-ended questions so that you don't limit customers' choices to your presumed answers when determining their preferred media sources. Use multiple choice when determining answers within a preset range of choices, such as preferred social media channels.

Along with finding out where customers go for their news, you'll also want to acquire some specific information about the person providing the response. This will help you narrow down your demographic and refine the audience you're targeting. As we've discussed, understanding your audience helps you further define and narrow in on the journalists you want to pitch. This should include acquiring gender and age range, at a minimum, so that you can distinguish behaviors within subsets to help you refine your pitch.

Once you have this information, sit down and carefully analyze it. What similarities do you see, either in terms of media channels or specific media outlets? This is where you want to start focusing your media efforts.

BUILD YOUR SURVEY

To view an effective sample survey to share with customers, visit freeprbook.com/tools.

TARGETING THE RIGHT MEDIA SOURCES

In addition to aligning your efforts with those of sales and marketing, and following your customers directly to the sources they're pointing you toward, you also want to put in some good old-fashioned research.

There are a lot of media channels out there. While all of them serve a purpose, the trick is to identify the channel that will provide the best platform for the story angle you're pitching. From there, you can begin to narrow your search for specific outlets.

While there is some room for variation, the following chart lays out the primary media channels at your disposal, and the areas and purposes they tend to lend themselves to best.

Media Channels & Outlets	Good for
Magazines (as well as their websites) Examples: *GQ, Cosmopolitan, People, WIRED, Forbes, Inc., Fortune*	General Magazines: • accessories • consumer goods • fashion • gifts • link juice • social proof Business Magazines: • B2B • business applications • consultants • SaaS • software
Newspapers (as well as their websites) Examples: *Chicago Tribune, Los Angeles Times, The New York Times, Wall Street Business Journal*	• creating credibility • high link authority • targeting Baby Boomers
Websites and mainstream blogs Examples: *Brit+Co, Mashable, PC Magazine, Refinery29 Techcrunch, The Verge*	• high throughput (easier to secure since they require lots of fresh content) • link juice • targeted traffic
Niche websites, blogs, and trade journals Examples: *Print Week, Variety*	• focus on very narrow audiences • small but passionate community • specific industry • targeted traffic

Media Channels & Outlets	Good for
Television programs Examples: *Good Morning America, Today, local news programs*	• demonstrating value • driving sales • social proof • video assets
Reviews Examples: *Appadvice, Consumer Reports, PC Magazine, Techcrunch, Tom's Lists*	• #1 way to drive sales and qualified traffic
Podcasts Examples: *"How I Built This"*	• reaching engaged niche audiences • word of mouth
Local media Examples: *business journals, city-level newspapers, local television and radio*	• community engagement • company morale • hiring • local businesses
Influencers and micro influencers Examples: *Kim Kardashian, Black Mom*	• driving awareness • niche products • sales

HACKS FOR IDENTIFYING THE RIGHT MEDIA OUTLET

Once you've narrowed in on certain channels that seem optimal for your purposes, you want to dig deeper and identify specific outlets. The surveys and conversations with colleagues mentioned above are a good start, but you'll want to look to other sources as well. Following are a few methods that have served us best.

LOOKALIKES AND COMPETITORS

Scouring the web to find the media outlets where lookalikes and competitors are appearing offers great insight into where your audience is going to consume content. It also gives you a line in to which journalists will likely welcome story pitches from you.

Conducting this type of research is as easy as searching Google News or BuzzSumo. BuzzSumo will charge a small price, but with this, you can enter in your competitor or lookalike's name and find out who's writing about them. Not only that, but you will also be able to access rankings, which provide information about readership. With this, you can figure out if your target audience is reading these articles, as well as the type of traffic the publication is driving.

A lookalike is a company that is in your industry and in some way similar to your company. Often, this similarity lies in culture and audience. A good litmus test for lookalikes is to ask yourself if you would like to partner with or in some way emulate this company. Likely, you would never want to partner with a competitor. Instead, your customers are choosing between your two companies. Ideally the lookalike should also be a company that has historically received a lot of media coverage within your industry.

If you are a makeup manufacturer creating a line of lipstick with a specific millennial audience in mind, Birchbox might be a lookalike. MAC would be a competitor, because they do what you do, which means some of your target customers are choosing between you and MAC.

If an outlet just covered MAC, they may not be ready to write a similar article again. Or, perhaps they are, providing you let the journalist know in very clear terms why your company is different. For example, you might write, "Unlike MAC cosmetics, we donate $5 from each lipstick to charity." Or, "Unlike MAC, our products are vegan."

When it comes to pitching based on lookalikes and competitors, it's critical to understand the nuance and context in which the company was covered. In other words, you can't just find the media hits—you also have to read through them. Was it a positive or negative article? Maybe the journalist lodged some sort of complaint about the lookalike. In this case, you have an opening by pointing out how your company is different or better. You don't want to just say, "We're the next Birchbox."

Alternatively, if the *Wall Street Journal* wrote about MAC's profit margins, that doesn't mean they'll be interested in a story about your company's new color line. It's the wrong context for the publication. This brings us to the next point: even reading through articles about lookalike and competing companies isn't enough. You want to take it a step further to research the journalist or column behind the article. What is their beat? What common themes do they cover? Be aware that some journalists specialize in critiques. These are probably not journalists you want to approach, regardless of how interested they might be in your company.

FINDING HIGH-TRAFFIC MEDIA OUTLETS

The number of people following an outlet's social media pages will usually give you a good idea of how popular the publication is and how many people they're reaching. Aside from sheer numbers, you also want to get an idea of how engaged the followers are. More important than the number of likes is how many times previous articles were commented on and shared. It's not an efficient use of your time to pitch publications that aren't getting a lot of traffic.

People new to pitching seem to think they need to start with small media outlets and build from there. Eradicate that notion. When it comes to PR, you want to go after the biggest, baddest targets. It doesn't take more time or effort to pitch to big versus small outlets. Keep slugging away until you get the big hit. *Think big.*

Start at the top of your media list in terms of engagement numbers and prestige, and work your way down. Even if you've never scored a single media hit before, pitch with confidence. The only thing you need to be on a level playing field with everyone else is an interesting, cohesive story angle that will appeal to the journalist's audience. This same rule of thumb applies equally to media outlets of all levels.

WEBSITES AND MAINSTREAM BLOGS

Websites and blogs are a great channel to explore

when you want to reach a highly targeted audience. The problem is, there are literally millions of them out there, some of which are great resources, and others that are collecting digital spiderwebs. To some degree, you can get an idea of how trafficked or authoritative a website or blog is by looking through it. However, this isn't a surefire strategy.

We like to use SimilarWeb, a web-traffic analysis tool that provides stats about the volume of visitors a site is receiving. SimilarWeb and other analysis tools will give you an approximation of how much traffic a site gets, as well as demographic information about its visitors. SimilarWeb is also a great tool for determining how to respond when a website or blog reaches out to you for free samples or services in exchange for promotion to their audience.

INFLUENCERS

In today's media landscape, you should consider influencers to be yet another media channel, and the equivalent of a journalist. Just like more traditional reporters, today's influencers are also people who help spread the word about noteworthy topics. Plus, influencers target those with a shorter attention span—and that sector of the audience is growing every single day. Particularly if your business is targeting customers who are millennials or younger, you need to be reaching out to influencers.

People are spending more and more time on YouTube, Twitter, Facebook, Snapchat, Instagram, LinkedIn, and B2B. The value of an individual like Gary Vaynerchuk, an influencer in the B2B space, holds far more weight for his audience than even a prestigious publication like the *Wall Street Journal* does. The same goes for the consumer space. People will put more credence into their favorite spokesmodel, actor, or musician when it comes to lifestyle trends than they will a magazine like *Vogue.*

None of this is to say that journalism is dead. It's not. However, social media represents a new and critical stream of media that must be utilized. Since influencers focus on niches, the right influencer often has the power to get you directly in front of hundreds of target customers who are ready and willing to act.

Another great benefit to influencers is that the vast majority of them are a one-person show, and just a

DM away. They are highly reachable and extremely open to partnerships and new product pitches. After all, that's what they're all about.

TRADE JOURNALS

Trade journals are often overlooked in the hunt for media outlets. Sure, these trade journals aren't as sexy as *Fortune* or *Forbes.* But they are often more effective than many mainstream publications and can be an incredibly valuable tool, particularly if you're a B2B company targeting a specific industry or vertical.

Whereas big commercial publications tend to cater to a very broad audience, trade journals attract readers who are highly interested and immersed in an industry. In other words, they are your target audience. If you identify the correct trade journal, a full 100 percent of readers represent potential customers. What other media outlet can offer such targeted exposure? The answer is none. By skipping over trade journals, you are leaving a potentially lucrative market completely untapped.

Due to the nature and scope of their audience, trade

journals are really the only outlet that will allow you to go into detail about your product or service. What a prime opportunity to tell your story from beginning to end and have your target audience read all about it!

More good news: trade journals are on the hunt for content just like every other media outlet. Not only that, but because they are generally overlooked in lieu of their mainstream counterparts, you aren't dealing with anywhere near the amount of competition you would at other media outlets. All of this means that trade journals' customers are more valuable to you and you're more valuable to them.

PRO TIP: USE REVIEWS AS A MEDIA CHANNEL

One of Adrian's all-time favorite hacks is utilizing reviews as a media channel. This will work well for anyone who is generating business for a product that already exists in the marketplace.

Begin by searching the name of your category plus the word "reviews" or "best." For example, if you have created an expense tracking app, you will Google "best expense tracking app." You will almost surely pull up a list of reviews for expense tracking apps. This shows you *exactly* what your customers are seeing and where they're going when they are in the market for a product just like yours. It's what people look up when they are interested and ready to pull the trigger on a product—in other words, they are your most valuable potential customers.

Ignore any links to blogs from your direct competitors and, instead, look for noteworthy review sites, such as *PC Magazine*. See who put together the review or product list, and reach out to that journalist. Reference the review you saw, and explain why your product is better or different. It's critical in this case to drive home your unique differentiator.

A couple of things can happen from here. Since the review is digital, the journalist might go in and update it. This is awesome, because you know for a fact that you'll come up at the top of searches for your product category. Or, if the journalist is really intrigued, they might opt to run an entire article on just your product.

WHO YOU WANT ON YOUR LIST

You'll want to include a selection of editors and journalists on your media list. This is what we call the top-down approach.

Since many media outlets now rely heavily on freelancers, it's important to identify a few department editors to pitch to. These editors read through the pitches, identify the ones that work for their publication, and assign them to freelance journalists. These editors represent the "top" of the top-down approach.

You'll also want to target some specific in-house journalists. These journalists represent the "down" in this approach, since they work under the editors. Every media outlet has journalists or contributors who write about different subjects. In some instances, certain outlets might have multiple journalists cover the same topic. For instance, there might be five writers covering the business beat at *Fortune* magazine. When this is the case, journalists generally have specific areas of expertise or interest within that broader topic. So, at *Fortune*, two of those five writers might specialize in the entrepreneurial space, two might cover the latest trends in marketing, and one might cover the financial industry. This means you need to make sure you're targeting journalists with as much specificity as possible. Just getting your pitch into the right department isn't enough.

PRO TIP: PUT YOURSELF OUT THERE

In addition to reaching out to journalists, you can also subscribe to a service called Help A Reporter Out (HARO; helpareporter.com), which alerts you when reporters have queries or are looking for specific information or sources. HARO sends out three emails a day with the latest requests. You can respond to these requests with a pitch to act as the information source.

BUILDING YOUR MEDIA LIST

Make sure that you have a specific email address for the journalists and editors you're pitching to. "Catch-all" department emails will likely land in a void, never to be seen again. You can do this in one of three ways, depending on how much money you do (or don't!) want to spend.

As you obtain media contact information, you'll want to build your media list. This is as easy as opening a spreadsheet; dividing it into categories according to the types of stories the journalists cover (for example, finance, investing, and trading); and logging the media outlet, journalist contact name, and contact information.

You can be even more sophisticated about your media list by storing it in a Customer Relations Management (CRM) software system. Our favorite is Pipedrive. A good CRM will allow you not only to log your media information, but also to categorize them according to profiles, such as targets, contacted, interested, and prospective.

This list will be your greatest resource. You will use it over and over again as you continue your PR efforts. Following are the three ways to build this list, based on your budget and time considerations.

BOOTSTRAP VERSION: DIY

There are two ways to create a DIY media list.

The first is to do a reverse media search. With this strategy, you will use Google News to search for articles that mention your lookalikes and competitors. Click on each article to see if it's relevant. If it is, simply identify the journalist. Often, you can get the journalist's contact information simply by clicking on their name. If not, you can use a readily available source like Twitter, LinkedIn, or Hunter.io to obtain their contact details.

If you already know the publications you want to reach out to, simply go to the publication and perform a search of lookalikes and competitors on their site. This will directly lead you to the journalists you want to be in touch with. The chances of these people wanting to hear from you and being interested in what you have to say are high.

What we really like about both of these strategies—aside from the fact they're free—is that reading through these articles will give you something specific to cite or relate to in an organic way when you reach out to the journalist. It's always good to be familiar with the work of reporters who cover your beat.

MIDRANGE VERSION: MEDIA DATABASES

If you are willing to spend a little bit of money in

order to save yourself some research time, you can utilize a media database (subscription service) to obtain journalist information. These services have a journalist database and are generally quite comprehensive. They will save you the effort and manpower of wading through articles and, instead, point you in the direction of those journalists who are most likely to fit the profile you're looking for.

Journalist database services like this generally cost an average of $500 per month; however, you can sometimes identify one for as inexpensive as $1,000 per year.

Another subscription service to consider is LinkedIn Pro. LinkedIn Pro allows you to directly email your contacts, which can be a simple but highly effective inroad to journalists' inboxes.

ELITE VERSION: OUTSOURCE

If time is of the essence and money isn't a huge concern, you can outsource a third party to build your list for you. These more boutique services range dramatically in price. However, with some research, you may be able to identify a PR or media consultant who will build this list for a price slightly cheaper than or comparable to a subscription journalist database.

> **BUILD YOUR MEDIA LIST**
>
> For more tips, tools, service providers, and templates to get your media list started, visit freeprbook.com/tools.

ORGANIZING YOUR MEDIA LIST

Now that you have your media contacts, you want to organize your list so that it's useful when the time comes to pitch. Create a spreadsheet with multiple tabs. These tabs will represent segments. You will want to have a segment for journalists or media channels who have covered direct competitors, a segment for journalists or media outlets who have covered companies similar to yours, and a segment for journalists or media outlets who cover your industry.

Next to each individual entry, include the journalist's name, the media company they work for, contact information, and any pertinent information you've uncovered that will be useful either to know or reference. This includes things like relevant articles, mutual acquaintances, and anything else that may connect the two of you or be a talking point later on down the line.

NEXT STEPS

Once you have done your homework and created a media list that includes the proper media outlet, section, and journalist to contact, it's time to step up to the mound and pitch.

CHAPTER FIVE

CREATE YOUR PITCH

All of the information you've collected so far has been building up to this moment. Now that you're armed with the specific information you need about your audience, story, and journalist, you have the parameters you need. You will want to keep all of these elements in mind as you weave them together into one cohesive product: your pitch.

EVERYTHING STARTS WITH THE PRESS RELEASE

Before we can even begin to strategize how to best approach media gatekeepers, we need to concentrate on creating a clear, concise, powerful press release. While it's true that journalists are accessible to you, it's also true that dozens—if not hundreds—of other people are also trying to get their attention on any given day. In the coming pages, we'll discuss several different strategies you can employ to ensure that you stand out from everyone else. First and foremost, at the very heart of this, is your press release.

Whether you've worked with a ton of press releases or none at all, chances are you think of them as an end-stage product. Press releases are generally regarded as a "hurrah" of sorts for crossing the finish line. Most people think, "We're ready to launch our product or service, so now the final step is to write the press release."

Amazon founder and CEO Jeff Bezos disagrees vehemently with this. At Amazon, product managers are required to write their press release as a first step. Press releases come before business plans, case studies, and the creation of the first line of code or a mock-up. The very first step of the creative process is a press release. Every single time.

At first, this sounds counterintuitive. However, what Amazon is actually doing with their press releases is reverse engineering. Most people think of press

THE PRESS RELEASE IS DEAD

There is a saying that goes, "The press release is dead—long live the press release." This pretty much sums up the press release in the modern era.

Before the internet took off, press releases served a very different purpose than they do today. Companies announced news through press releases, which they then put out on what is referred to as "the wire." Every day, editors and journalists—who have access to the wire—would reference these press releases as a critical part of their hunt for news.

Back then, there was more of a vetting process. Not everyone could release a press release and get it on the wire. This served as a barrier to entry. Thanks to the internet, today *anyone* can get a press release out there. This means there's a lot of junk, so press releases don't serve the purpose or hold the weight they once did. For a while, when paid press release wire sites were popular, they dominated Google's search results. Once Google realized this, they changed their algorithm so that press releases are now buried deep within search results.

Nonetheless, press releases are still important. Writing a press release will help you figure out what's interesting and relevant about your company. In this case, "relevant" refers to how your company is on trend and relevant to the media. Alternatively, it might show how you are different from everything else that's currently out there. You *must* be clear on this before you even think about pitching to journalists. If you can't write an interesting press release, you won't be interesting to journalists.

releases as a means to an end, but Bezos recognizes them for the powerful tool they are.

THE PRESS RELEASE AS A VISIONARY DOCUMENT

Press releases allow you to answer critical questions about your product—who, what, when, where, why (and, sometimes, how). Since press releases should not exceed a page, they also force you to be precise in your explanation. The final, very important ingredient of the press release recipe is that they have to be interesting. If they're not—well, who cares?

Bezos sees it this way: if you can't create an interesting press release, how are you going to make an interesting product? The press release also answers a lot of questions that you need to have a specific and intimate understanding of in order to create a product or service that works. You need to know who you are targeting, what problem you're solving, and why your solution is the best in the business. If you can't answer all of these questions in very clear terms, you probably shouldn't be creating the product in the first place. You've just saved yourself a lot of time, money, and effort.

While we agree with Bezos's line of reasoning, what we would also add is that a good press release will also serve as a powerful visualization tool. For internal purposes, a press release will make your product or service real, perhaps before it even exists.

CREATING A PRESS RELEASE

Your press release will consist of seven parts. To demonstrate what each element looks like, we'll use a fictional company called Lawntastic. Lawntastic is the Uber of yard maintenance. You open an app, select your services, and a gardener shows up to beautify and maintain your yard within the hour. Lawntastic is just launching its app, and they need to create a press release in preparation for the pitching process.

The Problem

You will begin your press release by defining the problem consumers are facing. In this case, the problem is that people can't afford their own gardener on a regular basis, yet they have little time to take care of their own yard maintenance. Every now and then, when they get really busy, they need some help that doesn't involve bringing a gardener in on a full-time, recurring basis.

Some products and services solve more than one problem, which is fine for the purposes of a press release. In this case, a secondary problem is that people often don't know who to hire for their gardening services and can only rely on the referrals of their friends. Often, these gardeners aren't available for hire or don't cover the neighborhood.

The Solution

Follow up the problem by immediately providing a solution. You will set forth the solution in simple terms. In the case of Lawntastic, the solution is that this new app makes getting your lawn mowed and bushes trimmed as easy as ordering an Uber, *and* it does so at an affordable cost and on an as-needed basis.

Data

The next paragraph of your press release should include some sort of data. From a journalistic standpoint, this is important because it establishes both the audience and the need for the story.

Data might include the citation of some research about market size, growth rate, dollars spent in this sector per year, or any other interesting, compelling facts.

This type of data also serves as a helpful visualization tool for you. If your research doesn't point to the fact that you have the potential to reach a growing or untapped market, what's the point of your product or service?

Quote

You will follow your data up with a quote. Generally speaking, this quote will be provided by a founder or the CEO of your company, but it can be given by anyone within your organization. The quote should be something inspirational like, "CEO Guy Grass says, 'This product has already revolutionized lawn care in our pilot audience, and we are excited to see it do the same for America.'"

You might also include a second quote from a customer, partner, or authoritative third party. If you are working on a product that doesn't yet have customers or a partner, you can always source a quote from the internet. For Lawntastic, this might include something like a quote from a noted home renovation expert or garden researcher, talking about the growth of on-demand apps in your industry or a related one. This second quote will provide additional credibility.

Call to Action

Your press release will end with a call to action. What do you want the reader to do next? Maybe you want them to download your app, in which case you would close with, "To download Lawntastic, visit the app store."

Summary

But, wait! There's more. You will actually lead your press release with a summary. While the summary leads the press release, it should be written last.

Now that you've thought through content and flow of your press release, you will succinctly summarize it in a single paragraph. This paragraph will be placed at the very beginning of your press release. It should explain who you are, what you do, and what you're launching.

This first paragraph is critical, because many journalists won't read beyond it. You have to make it count.

Headline

For much the same reason the summary is the final paragraph you'll create, the headline of your press release is the last element you'll write. Your headline has to wow, because if you—who knows your company better than anyone else—can't get directly to the most exciting part of your company or product, how can you possibly expect a journalist to? In the case of Lawntastic, you might write, "Lawntastic is disrupting the $6 billion lawn-care market."

It often takes several attempts to write a great headline. We find it's helpful to come up with a minimum of five options so that you have a selection to choose from.

Spoiler alert: this headline will serve dual purposes, as it will also be your email pitch subject line.

Headline	**Lawnstastic Launches the World's First Lawn Care on Demand Service to Offer Gardening Services with the Tap of a Button**
Sub-Headline (optional)	*Company is looking to disrupt the $77 billion lawn care industry with new app and marketplace*
Location and Release Date / Summary	NEW YORK, NY, April 1, 2019 – Lawntastic is announcing the launch of a new marketplace that will allow homeowners anywhere in North America to order lawn care services through an app. Services include grass cutting, aeration, fertilization, weed control, trimming bushes and trees. The app is now available from the Apple App Store.
Problem	Maintaining a lawn can be costly, time consuming, and inconvenient. Hiring a gardener can be a hit or miss experience. The average homeowner spends more than six hours a month simply maintaining their lawn. This despite the fact that there is no shortage of skilled workers in the US who are available to offer gardening services but lack the capital or business experience to start their own business.
Solution	Lawntastic will bridge the gap between vetted lawn care professionals looking for flexible work times and homeowners looking for cost effective, no-hassle lawn maintenance services. The services can be ordered as needed or using an automated schedule on a daily, weekly, or monthly basis. The workers are also fully insured.
Data and Market Facts	The lawn care market represents $77 billion in the US alone and is growing according to Turf Magazine. The gig economy is expected to reach of 26 million people this year and is growing at a rate of 7 percent as more and more people seek work flexibility and alternative sources of income.
Your Quote	"We're proud to be launching an innovative solution that will help make home owners' lives easier while creating new income sources for skilled workers across the United States," said, Johnny Appleseed, CEO of Lawntastic. "We're looking to Uber-fy an industry that has seen little innovation over the last century."
Influencer, Customer, or Partner Quote (optional)	"We've been using Lawntastic as part of their beta program for three months now. My lawn has never looked better and it's one less thing to worry about," said Montgomery Burns of Springfield, NY. "It's almost like having a full-time gardener, but without the high costs."
Closing and call to action	Lawntastic services start at as little as $29 for a basic package. The company is offering a free assessment to the first 1,000 customers to sign up. To learn more about Lawntastic visit TryLawntastic.com or download the app directly from the Apple App store.
Boilerplate	**About Lawntastic** Lawntastic offers the world's easiest lawn care service using a user-friendly app and vetted marketplace. Lawntastic is on a mission to make lawncare fast, affordable, and as easy as ordering an Uber. With more than 5,000 lawn care professionals (and growing) available on-demand, the company is looking to disrupt the $77 billion lawn care industry. To learn more, download the Lawntastic app from the Apple App store or visit www.trylawntastic.com.

CREATE YOUR OWN PRESS RELEASE

To access press release creation tools and a template to get you started, visit freeprbook.com/tools.

COMMON PRESS RELEASE PITFALLS

Many people commonly make a couple of deadly press release errors. The first and most egregious of these errors is failing to make a press release interesting. Whatever you do, don't just check off each section to get it done. Think through them. Spend some time. Imagine what your competitors are writing, and take a different approach that sets you apart.

People often fill their press releases with hyperbole. They exaggerate. Is your company really going to be bigger than Facebook? Do you really think you'll hit $1 billion sales in the first year? Journalists are seasoned professionals. They're not interested in what you're selling if you're full of hot air and inflate your numbers and claims.

Don't forget to share your press release with other members of your team or friends using an editing tool like Google Docs so they can make comments, suggestions, and do some editing and proofreading with "fresh eyes."

WHY YOUR PRESS RELEASE SHOULD BE ON THE WIRE ANYWAY

We began this chapter by talking about how the wire is no longer a useful tool. In many ways this is true. However, once you have finished sending your pitch to reporters (more on this in the following section), we still recommend that you get it up on the wire.

The wire today serves one valuable purpose, which many people are unaware of, and that represents a huge hack. Press releases sent using PRWeb are automatically filtered into LinkedIn. Anyone you mention in your press release—such as an investor, CEO, board member, or partner—will automatically be tagged, and their followers will be notified. This spreads the word about your company, product, and message. And, really, the purpose here is to spread news of your company far and wide.

The easiest way to publish your press releases is

through PRWeb.com. This service will distribute and track your press release with just a couple of clicks of the button.

WRITING YOUR PITCH

If you're reaching out to twenty different journalists, you don't have to write twenty different pitches. However, you *do* have to tailor your pitch to the situation at hand. This is where the segmented media list comes in handy (see chapter four). Generally speaking, a similar email can be sent to every journalist within a given segment. Obviously, you want to be extremely diligent about swapping out identifying information, specific references to previous articles, and any other identifying information.

Your subject line is critical—reporters' inboxes often look like a Twitter feed, with hundreds of emails coming in per day. You have a couple of options when it comes to composing the subject line of your pitch email. You may want to begin with the headline you wrote for your press release. With this strategy, you're giving the journalist a clear idea of what they'll find in your email and why it's compelling.

Another tactic we like is using a subject line that asks for the reporter's opinion or reads as a little more informal or personal. It could be something like "I'd love to get your opinion on this," or, "I thought you might like this." We track all of our open rates and have found this strategy to be successful.

You will begin your email by addressing the journalist by name. Start off with a sentence that lets them know why you are reaching out to them and believe the information you have to share will be of interest. For example, "I very much enjoyed your recent article about how fewer Americans have time for yard maintenance." Next, explain how that ties to your story pitch. Here you might write, "I thought you would be interested in a new solution that will make lawn care easier and accessible for the average American."

If you are a founder, CEO, or other high-level executive (or if you are crafting a pitch for company leaders to send), you can also start with something along the lines of, "Hi, Joe, I am the cofounder of the world's first on-demand lawn-care service app." This is yet another advantage to doing your own

PR. Emails like this demonstrate that a founder is excited about and invested enough in the idea to take time out of their busy schedule to personally reach out.

From here, you want to answer the question, "Who cares?" The goal is to hit a nerve. Refer to your press release, and pick out what you find to be the most compelling and attention-grabbing piece of information. For example, you might write something like, "Did you know the lawn-care industry is worth more than $2 billion? And we're positioned to completely change the way people take care of their lawns." Follow this up by demonstrating how you have market appeal and will bring an audience with you. It might look something like this: "Since we launched, we've had more than ten thousand beta users," or, "We've landed celebrity clients like Kim Kardashian."

Next, you will include four or five supporting statements or bullet points that convey your story angle. You are giving the journalist the story in a very succinct manner. *Remember, you're not actually writing the story for the journalist.* Instead, as the subject-matter expert or insider, you're giving the journalist an idea of your vision for what this story can be, along with the top-level information they need to understand why their audience will be interested in the topic. It's like the cliché about leading a horse to water. Ultimately, it's the horse's job to drink. But the easier you make it for the horse to find the water, the more likely it is he'll drink.

Let the reporter know if you will be providing images to go along with the story. This might seem like a minor detail, but images are not only worth a thousand words—they're also worth a thousand bucks. Great images help sell a great story, so don't be afraid to brag about your original or exclusive photography. This mention will serve as a dangling carrot. You don't want to actually include the high-res images (or even a link to them) in your initial pitch. However, in cases where you have truly extraordinary photos to show off or your product is better explained visually, you can embed (in other words, copy and paste) a web-resolution image so that it loads quickly. Do *not* attach large resolution files, as they need an extra step to open and download. That annoys most reporters.

Sign off by letting the reporter know there is an element of exclusivity to your pitch. For example, "I'd love to give you an exclusive sneak peek of the app," or, "We have collected some data that no one else has seen yet."

Finish up by letting the journalist know how you can be reached. We like to slip in our cell numbers with a note that the journalist can call our mobile at any time.

Finally, end by linking to your unreleased press release. We recommend using Google docs to host your press release before you officially post on a newswire to allow journalists to preview it. However, your email should be clear and compelling enough that the journalist doesn't have to open the press release (which many of them won't) in order to understand why this story is worth following up on.

Before you press send, read through your email and make sure you can answer yes to each of the following questions:

- Are you effectively conveying your desired points and why you're different or better?

- Will the story angle you're pitching help your company achieve its objectives?
- Is your pitch compelling and relevant to the journalist's audience so that they are likely to say yes?

Once you are satisfied that you can answer each of these questions with a definitive and enthusiastic yes, you're ready to hit send.

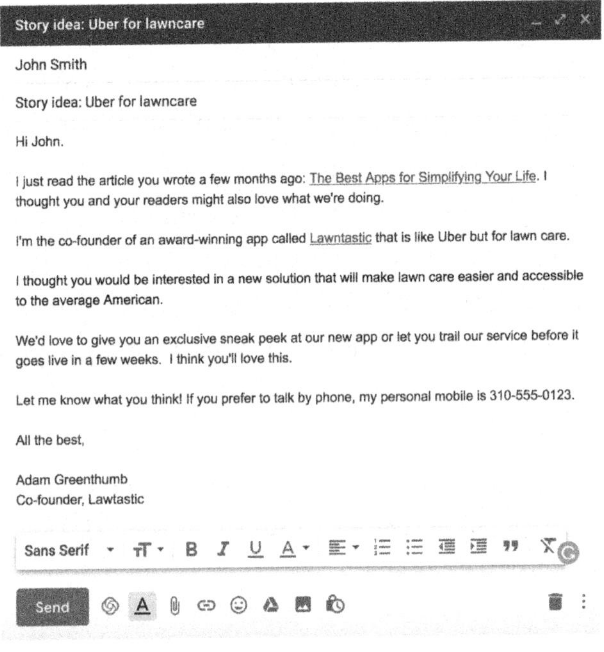
Story idea: Uber for lawncare

John Smith

Story idea: Uber for lawncare

Hi John.

I just read the article you wrote a few months ago: The Best Apps for Simplifying Your Life. I thought you and your readers might also love what we're doing.

I'm the co-founder of an award-winning app called Lawntastic that is like Uber but for lawn care.

I thought you would be interested in a new solution that will make lawn care easier and accessible to the average American.

We'd love to give you an exclusive sneak peek at our new app or let you trail our service before it goes live in a few weeks. I think you'll love this.

Let me know what you think! If you prefer to talk by phone, my personal mobile is 310-555-0123.

All the best,

Adam Greenthumb
Co-founder, Lawtastic

> **WRITE YOUR PITCH**
>
> To view a pitch template that has proven to work, and for more pitch-writing guidance, visit freeprbook.com/tools.

EMAIL BROADCASTING

Generally speaking, it's best to "sniper" journalists—in other words, to reach out to them on a personal, individual basis. However, every now and then, it's necessary to reach out to several journalists in one fell swoop. This tactic should be limited to specific situations, such as a major company announcement or acquisition that is time sensitive. When such instances arise, email broadcast tools come in handy. Broadcasting allows you to send up to fifty emails with the click of a single button. We like Yesware to do mail merge, although there are several good email broadcast systems available online.

NEXT STEPS

If you've followed the Free PR strategy thus far, chances are you'll be in direct contact with journalists soon. Next up, we'll take a look at what to expect once your pitch has been sent out into the world.

CHAPTER SIX

WORKING WITH JOURNALISTS

In some cases, you may hear back from a journalist based on your pitch email. Often, it's necessary to follow up on your initial email. In fact, following up usually constitutes the vast majority of the pitching process, and it is when your most significant contact with journalists will occur.

Following up doesn't mean that your pitch didn't work, or the journalist has rejected your idea. It simply means you're dealing with people who are on a lot of tight deadlines and have very full inboxes. In this chapter, we'll look at some best practices for follow-up and next steps.

CULTIVATE YOUR STYLE

Both of us have been extremely successful in pitching stories to top-echelon journalists across all media channels. However, we have different—and somewhat conflicting—styles for doing so. There are plenty of other public relations experts out there whose opinions differ from ours, and they've also found success.

As an answer to this, we have decided to include both of our strategies, each of which has landed huge media hits. Take what works for you, and feel free to experiment with your own personal pitching style.

At the end of the day, you have to find a strategy that works for you, feels comfortable, and bears the journalist's situation in mind. Whatever strategy you use, it's crucial that you find the balance between bringing your pitch to the journalist's attention and respecting their time and tight deadlines.

ADRIAN'S PR STYLE: THE 1-2-3 PUNCH

Before we start, I want to share some news with you. Getting PR is hard. It's called earned media for a reason. It's not uncommon to have a 5 percent closing rate. That means you might have to send out one hundred pitches to get five good story placements. Know that you are not the only one; this is a common experience.

To help even out the odds, I like to hit journalists with what I call the 1-2-3 punch. This involves strategically contacting them through multiple channels. Obviously, harassing a journalist is not going to net you the results you want. It will just make you look like a pest. Always remember that you're dealing with busy people on deadlines. However, you can follow up in such a way that you can turn the journalist's attention toward your pitch and pique their interest. Here's how it works.

EMAIL YOUR PITCH

Congratulations! At this point, you've already completed step one of the 1-2-3 punch by sending your initial pitch email. Your pitch was personalized, short, and relevant, and now it's sitting in the journalist's inbox, and easy for them to reference when you follow up.

TWITTER

Most journalists rely heavily on Twitter because of its immediacy and accessibility. Journalists need to be in touch and accessible for story ideas and sources, and Twitter is one of the primary outlets they mine for this purpose. In fact, I work with several journalists whose preferred way to receive pitches is via Twitter.

Nonetheless, unless you know a journalist's specific preferences, you should always start with email. Twitter will represent your second punch. Before you begin tweeting for PR purposes, make sure that your Twitter profile is professional. This means a profile that uses your own name (or some version of it), a great headshot for your profile picture, a mention of your company in the bio, and making sure the account is used solely for professional communication. If, for some reason, this is not possible, you can also tweet journalists directly from your corporate Twitter account.

Begin by following the journalist if you're not already. Ideally, you will have the ability to direct message a journalist on Twitter. DMs are great because you can see if your message has been read or not. If you don't have the ability to DM, it's okay to use an @mention as an alternative approach.

I generally tweet a journalist within an hour of sending the pitch to ensure that it's fresh in their minds and (at least relatively) near the top of their inbox. The goal from here is to start a back-and-forth conversation. This doesn't always happen, but be ready to engage in case the opportunity presents itself.

FOLLOW UP ON EMAIL

I've done a lot of surveying about journalists' email volume and habits. On average, they receive approximately one hundred emails per day. Since it's their job to read them, they will likely open your email, providing your subject line is well crafted and your pitch is short, to the point, and targeted.

However, it's usually a quick read. Often, journalists will flag an email that's of interest to return to it later. This is when emails get lost in the shuffle.

If I haven't heard back from a journalist after my first email or Twitter contact, I will send a second email a day or two later. In my experience, the second email has a higher response rate because the journalist often apologizes for not answering yet. They may pass or express interest at this point. My follow-up email goes something like this.

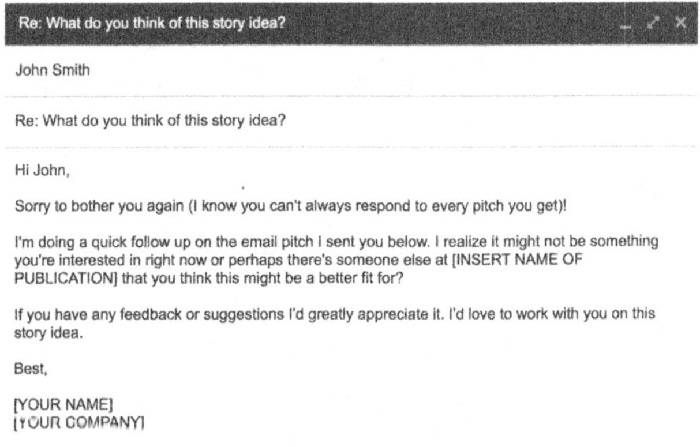

Re: What do you think of this story idea?

John Smith

Re: What do you think of this story idea?

Hi John,

Sorry to bother you again (I know you can't always respond to every pitch you get)!

I'm doing a quick follow up on the email pitch I sent you below. I realize it might not be something you're interested in right now or perhaps there's someone else at [INSERT NAME OF PUBLICATION] that you think this might be a better fit for?

If you have any feedback or suggestions I'd greatly appreciate it. I'd love to work with you on this story idea.

Best,

[YOUR NAME]
[YOUR COMPANY]

PHONE

Your bonus round of contact is the telephone, but only when the journalist specifically requests more information in response to one of your first three outreach attempts. While I had a lot of success using the telephone as a primary mode of pitching ten years ago, things have changed. More journalists work from home now, use their personal mobile phone, and are constantly on deadline. This means that pitch calls are more invasive than helpful as opposed to the digital modes of contact at your disposal.

I will use the phone as a primary point of contact in the very rare and specific case that I have a story that is custom-designed for a specific journalist, and that I know they'll love. This almost always means that I have a preexisting relationship with the journalist, which is very different from cold-calling.

MOVING ON

All of your pitches won't get bites. In fact, a lot of them won't. That's okay. Be diligent in your follow-up, but also know when it's time to stop. You are much better off letting a pitch go than annoying a journalist. Part of your goal with each pitch is to cultivate a relationship with the reporter, not to pester them to the point that they never want to hear from you again or, worse yet, block you.

BEING PERSISTENT VERSUS PESTERING

One of the mistakes people make is ruining a relationship with journalists before it even begins by pestering them about a pitch that clearly isn't going to work. Enthusiasm is great, and you do want to be the squeaky wheel, but you also have to know when to stop. That's why I like the 1-2-3 punch method so much—it puts you out there, but at a reasonable level that will serve your budding relationship with a reporter over the long run.

As you become more seasoned at pitching and finding that balance becomes more innate, you can begin to get more creative. I've had this pay off for me in big ways, including an appearance on *The Big Idea with Donny Deutsch.* This CNBC show used to draw about three million viewers back when network television was far more important than it is today. I was determined to get DNA11 on it. And I did. After being rejected six times by the producers.

Each time I was rejected, I refused to be deterred. I framed it as being one rejection closer to acceptance. I emailed them, I called them, I did everything I could to get their attention. Nonetheless, I got the same answer every time. "You're Canadian," they would tell me. "We don't accept Canadians on our show."

Most people would have given up after one or two attempts. Almost everyone would have given up after three attempts. Not me, though. I had my eye on the prize, and I wasn't going to be deterred.

I constantly kept my eyes open for inroads and opportunities, knowing that if I looked hard enough, sooner or later I would find one that worked. One day, I saw that the CEO of a home-furnishing company called Umbra was a guest on the show. I knew damn well that he was from Toronto. *He was Canadian!*

Thrilled, I rushed to email the producer. "Hey!" I said. "I just noticed a Canadian was on the show. I guess you can have me on now!" No response. I decided it was time to go all in. So, I emailed the vice-president of NBC (CNBC's parent company), but not at his work address. I did some research, found his university alumni email address, and contacted him there. I figured he would receive a lot fewer emails at this address, which would allow mine to stand out. In the email, I told him the story of my company in a really enthusiastic, colorful way, and included the joke about being from Canada. I didn't ask if I could be on the show, though—instead, I made the smaller ask to be introduced to the show's producers.

An hour later, he forwarded my email to a producer—the same producer who had told me no so many times. I immediately received a response from her: "We'd love to cover you."

It can be argued that I bullied my way onto the show. However, I did all of this with a joking demeanor, and was careful to read the producers. I could tell they were amused with my persistence, so I kept on going. Had I sniffed out an air of true annoyance, I would have pulled back and used a different strategy.

Remember that you're dealing with people. Be smart, and play by the rules—but also, use your instincts and don't be afraid to break the rules when you sense the opportunity for a big payoff.

CAMERON'S PR STYLE: DIFFERENTIATE YOURSELF

Want to know how to capture the attention of reporters these days? You have to look beyond just sending emails. While it's quick and easy to type a note and tap the send key, everyone else is doing the same thing. Your message can easily get buried amid the hundreds a reporter receives on a given day. Pitching with email alone gives you a 1 percent chance of being seen.

Picking up a phone and calling a reporter, on the other hand, could make all the difference between having your pitch heard or ignored. These days, most of us only receive a handful of calls per day, primarily from people we know who want to say hello. By calling a reporter, you increase your odds of catching them by about 20 percent.

FIVE WAYS TO GET A REPORTER'S PHONE NUMBER

1. Database tools such as CISION and other PR databases sometimes include phone numbers for individual journalists. Despite this, phone numbers are still becoming increasingly difficult to find, since journalists work from remote locations or use their personal mobile phones and are hesitant to provide this information.

2. LinkedIn users can export their contacts' data, which includes phone numbers when provided. Go to Settings and request a data archive of your connections. You will then download an Excel spreadsheet, which includes phone numbers, email addresses, job titles, and more.

3. Many journalists—especially freelancers—have personal sites. These sometimes list their phone number under About Me or Contact Me sections.

4. Call the publication's main number and ask. If you're extra polite, sometimes they will provide a direct extension. Alternatively, you can try using the dial-by-name feature if they have an automated attendant.

5. Email signatures often include a phone number. If you happen to receive an email with this information, you're in luck! After all, the journalist would not include it in their signature if they minded your using it.

Successful PR requires separating yourself from competitors. You want to think big, be fearless, and zig when others zag. Using the phone as your primary mode of communication is one way to stand out. Not only have you reduced your odds of being ignored, but you can make a more personal and memorable connection by talking to someone rather than writing. This approach makes them feel as if they are being pitched to as an individual rather than as part of an email that was copied, pasted, and delivered to hundreds of people.

When calling a reporter with a pitch, I always start by saying, "Do you have a couple of minutes? I have a great story for you." The answer will generally be either, "Sure, go ahead," or, "No, I'm too busy." Never once has a journalist given a flat-out "no" to a potentially good story.

If the person is busy, I ask if it's okay for me to call back, and then I give them a specific time, like Thursday morning or Monday afternoon. Again, no one ever says, "No, I'm never available." In all likelihood, you'll be able to pitch your idea at some point.

When you deliver your pitch, begin with the conversational version of your story's headline. Follow that up with the four or five key points of your story angle. It should only take you a couple of minutes to deliver the rough sketch of your idea. With this, you've completed your primary job: you've offered your idea to the person on the other end of the line.

Now it's your turn to let the journalist ask questions and engage with you on the topic. Be helpful as you present your angle, but try to refrain from doing all of the talking. It's a bit counterintuitive, but the more you talk, the less chance you have of landing the story. The real key here is to get the journalist talking. People don't want to feel sold; they want to feel as if they made a conscious decision to do whatever it is you want them to do.

I like to finish by asking the journalist directly, "What do you think about turning this into a story?"

If they like the idea and are ready to move forward with it, I ask if they would prefer that I give them more information now or that we set up a longer interview for another day.

Sometimes ideas are rejected. That's okay, too. In fact, you should be prepared for that. If the journalist has already written on the topic, doesn't see it as a match for their readers, or even plain old doesn't like the idea, you're still walking away with valuable feedback. This information can be put to use at a later date. The biggest bonus to this method is that regardless of the outcome, you have now begun to establish a relationship with this reporter, which may very well pay off in other ways down the line.

MEDIA COMMUNICATION CHANNELS

As you can see, you have options for how you go about communicating with journalists. As you begin to figure out the strategy that works best for you, consider some pros and cons about the various communication methods available to you.

Communication Channel	Pros	Cons
Email	Most journalist prefer to be pitched this way Trackable and measurable (opens and clicks) Scalable, easy to do, low friction Can easily add images, visuals, and links to more information	Very noisy; journalists get 100 or more pitches a day, so it's hard to stand out If you don't do this right, you can go to the spam box, or even be blocked by journalists
Social platforms / Direct messages (Twitter, LinkedIn, Instagram, etc.)	Many journalists (especially in tech) keep this channel open and actually prefer to receive pitches this way Forces you to keep your pitches short, informal, and conversational, which are all good things Some platforms, like Twitter, let you see when a DM has been delivered or even read Especially strong channel for reaching social media influencers	Careful not to "cross the line" into accounts that are clearly designed for personal rather than professional use Some journalists don't want to be reached this way (and will often tell you so in their profile), so make sure to respect their wishes Can be more time consuming to pitch individuals using social media as compared to email
Phone	Very few people pitch by phone, so if you can get someone on the line, you will stand out It's personal; if you pitch well the journalist will detect your passion It's conversational; you can really connect with the journalist and answer their questions or receive feedback on the spot It's always great to connect by phone once a journalist has expressed interest	It's disruptive; you can annoy time-starved journalists if you call them at the wrong moment It's difficult to find a journalist's number; most journalists work off-site It's time consuming (between finding the correct number, calling, etc.) Not visual; you can't send links, images, etc. by phone
Physical letters / Samples	You can stand out in a good way If your product is good, the journalist will love to get samples It's personal and makes people feel special It's trackable, which makes it easier to follow up	It can be expensive, - so save this for super VIP journalists and influencers Time consuming and harder to scale

NEXT STEPS

We've spent the past several chapters learning how to strategically grab the media's attention. Once you've put these skills to use and successfully landed a hit, it's time to move on to the next stage—preparing to meet with the media and share your story.

MASTER THE INTERVIEW PROCESS

CHAPTER SEVEN

TELEVISION AND PODCAST INTERVIEWS

Congratulations! This is what you've been waiting for: the chance to tell the world (or at least a sector of it) about your company.

While getting to this point is a big step forward, don't forget that you haven't accomplished your mission quite yet. One of the biggest mistakes people make is getting lazy or complacent once an interview is locked and loaded. You still have lots of work to do between the time your story is accepted and when it's written or recorded.

Your preparation process and interview tactics will vary, depending on the media channel you're working with. We'll start off with television and podcasts, which can be an intimidating scenario to walk into for those who are new to the experience.

DO YOUR HOMEWORK

This should go without saying, but plenty of people fail to research the show they are appearing on beforehand. Don't fall into this category. As you begin looking at media with a more critical eye, you'll begin to notice that it's actually quite clear when someone steps into an interview without first having done their homework. And not in a good way.

Remember that one of the most important elements of your research thus far was pitching your story in such a way that it would appeal to the journalist's audience. Now you have to deliver intriguing and compelling content. The best way to do this is to understand the media channel on which you will be appearing. This will provide great insight into what makes the audience tick.

If you're appearing on a television show or podcast, watch or listen to it a few times to understand both the format and the reporters. If you're being interviewed for a print or digital publication, read through past articles that are somehow related to your story, as well as articles the person interviewing you has written.

Learn who the audience is. Understand the tone and the style of the show or publication. Is it casual or serious? What is the journalist's demeanor or slant? Imagine appearing on a show like *The Colbert Report* without understanding that the host was playing a satirical role. How off-message and out of rhythm would you be? This is an extreme example, but the point applies regardless of the media channel you're appearing on or interviewing with.

Cameron once did an interview with someone who was very businesslike and did everything by the book. Then, all of a sudden, in the middle of the interview, he threw a sarcastic little jab at Cameron. "Wow. What a jerk," Cameron thought. The reality is, this was a normal part of the interviewer's shtick. Cameron was thrown because he hadn't prepared enough to realize that he should have been ready and waiting for it. He also should have been prepared to respond in kind.

Some interviewers will get you talking and then let you go. Interviews like this are ripe with opportunity because you have the room to tell your story and take it in the direction you want it to go without being cut off or led. Then, there are interviewers who will cut you off after every sentence, and make you work to get your message out.

It's your job to know in advance what to expect on a particular show and with a certain interviewer. The more research and preparation you do, the better chance you have of conveying your story the way you want it told.

PREPARE YOUR TALKING POINTS

Most often, your audience will not listen to your interview the entire way through from beginning to end. If they do, it will likely be because they heard a clip they found compelling. These clips are known as sound bites—short snippets of your interview that the media outlet will use for various purposes, such as promotion or "coming up next" segments.

These sound bites are taken from the most compelling parts of your interview. You want to talk with these sound bites in mind, particularly in video and audio interviews, when your time is short and your interview may be edited down.

Prepare four or five core talking points prior to your interview, just like you did for each story angle. Before the interview, go over these points again and again. Use Post-it notes to write each one out, and practice saying them. During the interview, use whichever point is most appropriate in response to the journalist's question. For instance, if one of your core talking points is about franchising, then you need to repeat the words "franchise," "franchising," "franchisors," "franchise partners," and "franchise territory" multiple times so that one of those terms will survive the cutting-room floor.

You'll also want to practice repeating the information in a reporter's question and incorporating it into your answer, particularly in the case of television. If a reporter asks if you think that you can really double your business in three years, don't just answer, "Yes," or, "I do." If the question is cut, those words are dangling out there as non sequiturs. Instead, answer like this: "You can double your business in three years." No, this isn't how we talk in a conversation, but television and podcast interviews aren't a real conversation; they're an artifice designed to look natural.

DON'T BE INTIMIDATED

Let's be honest. Appearing on television, YouTube Live interviews, podcasts, or anything else of this nature can be intimidating. *Especially* if it's live.

Some years ago, a company Cameron worked for handed out blue wigs for fans to wear during the Vancouver Canucks playoff hockey games. It was a marketing stunt designed to get publicity. As a result, two TV stations came to Cameron's office for a live remote interview—at the same time. Initially, there were a lot of nerves about how two simultaneous segments would be handled.

When the two crews arrived, it turned out that some of them had gone to college and worked together before. They were chummy. In fact, they helped each other haul their equipment onto the roof of the building for the shoot.

In that moment, we realized something about the media: they're normal people like the rest of us. That experience demystified them.

As for the blue-wig stunt, it was a hit. Cameron's company was featured in sixty-seven separate media stories in just a two-week period.

BE READY TO ROLL

The rule of thumb with television or any other form of media is that when a journalist calls, you should drop everything.

Television, in particular, is a very opportunistic medium. There are slow days when no big news is breaking. You'll never hear this, though. A television program will never announce, "There won't be any programming today, because there isn't any news." Instead, they create the news. This is why you have to constantly seek and reach out to television journalists to see if they're looking for a good story.

Local news programs are always looking for last-minute content to fill programming gaps. Slow news days aside, stories die frequently and for any number of reasons. This represents a major opportunity for you. If you establish a relationship with a news producer and are at some point able to get that producer out of a bind, they are almost guaranteed to come back to you again.

The opposite is also true; television moves quickly, and it won't wait for you. One of our clients learned this lesson the hard way when they missed their opportunity. They received a call from a television producer who wanted to do a piece on the company. When the call came, they were too absorbed with business and meetings to address the situation immediately. Instead, they told the journalist they would get back to him. And they did—thirty-six hours later.

When they finally got around to calling back, the journalist explained that the ship had sailed. This company let the opportunity they had worked so hard for slip right through their fingers. As is often the case, the journalist's story was time-sensitive. Unfortunately, our clients didn't understand that the media operates on deadlines. This happened to be a television show, which has some of the tightest deadlines in the business. In this case, they were producing a segment for a news story that afternoon.

Cameron also learned this lesson the hard way. About a year and a half ago, a very famous blogger wanted to interview him, but Cameron didn't have time to meet in person. Instead, they tried Skyping, but their connection was unstable. That was the end of that. Cameron has spent the past eighteen months playing catch-up, trying to get back on the blogger's radar. Unfortunately, her needs and desires have changed. Cameron likely missed his opportunity. Looking back, he understands that when their Skype session crashed, he should have jumped on a plane to New York and gone to see her in person.

These tight deadlines are yet another reason you should always include your mobile number in pitches. That way, you're reachable if there's an urgent deadline. One time the *Conan O'Brien Show* contacted Adrian at 7:00 p.m. because one of his customers (Elijah Wood of *Lord of the Rings* fame) was a guest. They wanted a picture we had on file of Elijah with our product. If Adrian had missed that call, an incredible—and very time-sensitive—opportunity would have disappeared into thin air. PR is not a nine-to-five game. You have to be available when the opportunities come in and turn around requests quickly.

While this book is about how to contact the press, when they contact you, they're handing you what you want on a silver platter. With a single call, they're saving you perhaps a month—or more—of time and effort landing a story. It's no exaggeration to say that it's a gift when the media calls you, and you want to accept that gift immediately and without exception.

Although each branch of the media works on a different schedule, one rule always applies: if someone from the press calls you, drop everything. You have no idea if that magazine story will run in a month, or if that journalist is scrambling to get a last-minute quote to round out this month's issue, which goes to press at the end of the day.

ON YOUR HOME TURF

There are a number of things you need to do before a camera crew comes to your office to shoot a segment or interview you. Some of these are common sense, and others might not be so intuitive.

Setting the scene at your office is your responsibility. The TV crew isn't concerned about promoting your business. They just want to do their job and go home. It's up to you to think about how you want your business to appear to the public—to your audience—and then it's up to you to create the right optics to provide the image you want to project.

Prepare ahead by making sure the space where the crew will be filming is free of clutter. Desks should be clean, and any random items around the office should be carefully stashed away and out of sight.

You might suggest to the interviewer and camera crew that you use a well-lit space that features a large company logo and an energetic backdrop of busy workers. Have any employees who might appear on camera dress in a way that represents your brand and culture.

Also, make sure those background workers know they can—and should—conduct business as usual. A sense of buzz and busyness sends a great message about your company and should not be stifled for the cameras.

PODCAST PREP

While you may go to a studio for a podcast appearance, chances are you'll be calling in. Rare as they are these days, you want to use a landline when interviewing. Skype and mobile connections can cut out and drop, which is not something you want to contend with in the middle of an interview. Most importantly, find a quiet place. You don't need dogs barking or kids yelling in the background.

The good news with podcasts is that you don't have to get camera ready. The challenge is that your voice is your only tool. If you listen closely to morning radio hosts, you'll notice they speak with a lot of high energy. This is no accident. Radio hosts *have* to bring this sort of energy if they want to invigorate commuters on their way to work. Think of these radio hosts when you go into radio and podcast interviews. You want to mimic that high level of enthusiasm and excitement about your message.

The pitfall to podcasts is that if you lack enthusiasm or energy, this medium will magnify that. So, whatever you do, *don't* wake up twenty minutes before your slot and think a cup of coffee will perk you up and get you ready to roll. It won't. Instead, try doing twenty jumping jacks or go for a run to get your pulse pumping. Do drink some warm tea infused with honey or lemon before you record to soothe your vocal chords and calm your voice. As basic as it sounds, have a glass of water within reach.

During the interview, try standing rather than sitting to increase your clarity of thought and the strength of your voice. When you stand, you're more likely to speak from your diaphragm, which will make you sound livelier and more authoritative. Believe it or not, poor posture and slouching will translate over the airwaves. The same is true of your expression, so smile! It will come through in the sound of your voice and will help the listener to better connect with you and your message.

ARRIVE EARLY

When you are going to a studio for a television or podcast appearance, always arrive thirty minutes before your call time. This is not just about being prepared for traffic delays; it's about leaving time for all of the prepping you need to do before you appear on camera. You'll want to look at the set and get a feel for the people. Do vocal exercises if that is part of your process. Have a glass of tea with lemon and honey to relax your vocal chords. You probably want to avoid coffee. It might get you wired, and jittery isn't the image you want to project on air. You want to present yourself as calm and comfortable so that the audience can connect with you.

Talk to people around the studio or even the interviewer if you can. Often, they'll have good advice that will put your nerves at ease. If you are appearing on television or a video segment, ask where you should look as you talk. Sometimes they'll want you to look directly at the interviewer, other times at the camera, and still other times back and forth between the two. Any specific information you can gather will make your interview much smoother and more enjoyable.

Arriving early also potentially gives you the opportunity to establish a rapport with the interviewer. Engaging in a little banter can ease the tension of meeting someone new on air when you're already nervous. The sooner you develop that chemistry, the smoother the flow of the interview once the cameras start rolling.

A lot of people are nervous about talking to the interviewer beforehand or are unsure what to say. Talk about something you know you have in common: the show. Break the ice by talking about a prior show or interview the reporter conducted. This also establishes that you know something about the show and the person you'll be speaking with. Adrian likes to ask the interviewer for details about the audience that he may not be aware of in order to frame his answers so they are most relevant to the audience.

Also, use your time before the show to find out what to expect at the *end* of the show. To avoid an awkward exit, clarify when you should get up to leave the interview before it even begins. Don't make any assumptions. There is no more surefire way to look like an amateur than by getting up while the host is doing a wrap-up or when you're supposed to be making friendly banter as the show fades into a break.

LOOKING POLISHED ON CAMERA

When you arrive at the studio for a television interview, ask if you can go into makeup—that's where the on-camera talent will be. Particularly if you're a man, the idea of having makeup applied might feel uncomfortable. Just know that the lights will wash you out, and your nose and forehead will look shiny without it. Is that really the look you want to show the world? (Also, the lights give off a great deal of heat, so be prepared to get toasty.)

And a reminder from someone who learned this lesson the hard way: don't forget to take your makeup off after the interview is over. Cameron rushed out of a Bloomberg TV interview one time and went directly into a meeting. He walked down several avenues of Manhattan without realizing he was still in full makeup!

This might sound like common sense, but it bears mentioning: avoid getting a haircut the day of your

TV appearance. Get it cut a few days in advance so that it doesn't look like you just got it trimmed twenty minutes before going on air.

Wear neutral colors like navy blue or any shade of gray, and opt for solids or subtle patterns like herringbone. Do *not* wear pinstripes. Pinstripe patterns have a strange effect on camera and create what's known as a moiré pattern—in other words, they look like blurry lines onscreen. Also avoid wearing white because it can wash you out, and it comes off too bright under the lights, which throws off the camera's sensors. Even with high-definition, some tiny prints pixilate onscreen, which creates a glowing effect that is terribly distracting to the eye. If you are wearing a suit jacket, sit on the bottom of it to keep it from riding up and bunching around your shoulders while you are seated.

It's important to prepare for this ahead of time because, if you don't, last-minute calls have to be made that might not work to your benefit. For example, Adrian's DNA11 cofounder wore a white shirt under a leather jacket on one of their first television interviews on the Discovery Channel. As a result, he had to zip the jacket all the way up to his neck to cover up the white shirt on air. He ended up looking like he was an extra on *Star Trek*.

Why are we mentioning such seemingly minor details? Because the idea is to bring attention to your message, not your wardrobe, skin, or hair. Viewers won't actively notice when you do things right—but they *will* notice when they are done incorrectly.

IS IT LIVE?

When it comes to podcasting, you can rest assured that your interview will be recorded. Television could be live, live-to-tape, or edited before it airs. If you're under the impression that a director is going to holler "Cut!" so you can take another stab at a sentence you butchered, then you're in for a harsh reality check when you learn the show is being recorded live—even if it won't be broadcast until later that day.

In the world of live TV, you get one take and then it's over.

Even if the show will be edited, nobody will invite

you into the editing booth to offer your input as they cut the segment. So, while you may have three minutes of footage during which you talk clearly, there's nothing to say they won't use the thirty seconds of you stammering as you try to remember the name of something.

PROMPTS

Want to know a secret? Those Post-it notes we recommend you make to help you practice before the show taping? Cameron also keeps one in his pocket to refer to just before filming begins. A quick review before going on air helps him remember what he wants to say in the interview. Sometimes he even has a large flip chart in his line of sight, resting near the camera. This chart acts like cue cards.

Many people feel that prompts are cheating. No one will mind if you use prompts—after all, reporters use teleprompters! Besides, the better you come across on air, the better the show looks.

At the end of the day, this is still entertainment.

Having said that, nobody will offer to have your

five talking points put on a chart for you. That's on you, and it's something you need to consider well in advance of your interview.

Also, if you're someone who feels more comfortable knowing what's coming, you can try to ask the reporter (or producer—whomever you're corresponding with to set up the interview) for the questions that are likely to come up during your segment. You certainly don't want to have a deer-in-headlights look, nor do you want to glance at the ceiling in search of an answer. Just know that many reporters won't share those questions, so the sooner you can get comfortable handling whatever questions are thrown to you, the better you'll do in interviews.

Some people speak more authentically off the cuff, and preparing ahead of time makes them sound rehearsed. Everyone is different, so just figure out what works best for you—which often comes through trial and error.

No matter how comfortable you are, it's still possible to get thrown when a quirky question is fired in your direction. Reporters have asked us questions like what our superpower is, or what our most embarrassing moment was. Who thinks about these things, anyway? But sometimes they do come up, mostly as a means of humanizing the interviewee and helping them establish a rapport with the audience. These questions can be helpful, but they can also throw you off your rhythm and message. Since you can't really prepare for these moments, just keep doing interviews, practice your talking points, and gain more experience in these settings.

GET YOUR POINT ACROSS

Podcasts often give you some freedom in terms of time. You can linger on your answers for longer than you can in a television or video interview, and the dialogue often feels more conversational. However, don't get distracted by that and forget to weave your core points into your answer. The sense of time and conversation you have on podcasts can often work against you. It's important to remain on your game and hit all of the topics you want to.

With television, there is usually more of a sense of urgency. It is a medium that moves quickly, and you will typically only have between thirty and sixty seconds to make your point—ninety, if you're lucky. This means you need to know your talking points inside and out, and you have to be able to articulate them clearly and succinctly. Talk in sound bites, and do not use filler words like "uh" or "um." When necessary, it's your job to lead the interview in order to get your message across to the audience. The journalist may not ask you the questions you want to answer, so be prepared to bring the interview back to your core message.

Whereas podcasts are rarely edited, television shows usually are. Since you have no control over how the interview is edited, it's critical that you repeat your talking points again and again. Sure, it might sound redundant on set, but when the audience watches or listens to the segment, they'll likely only hear what you say once.

Television is not a venue that values nuance. You're not looking to show off your vocabulary or to showcase your breadth of knowledge. The job requires a sledgehammer that continually pounds away on one thing. And while this is certainly an unnatural way of speaking, it will become second nature the more you practice it. The savviest speakers are able to talk in this fashion unconsciously because they understand what the finished product sounds like.

BE PRESENT

Whereas television keeps you present in the moment, it can be easy to get lazy during a podcast interview—especially after you have a few under your belt. Although most podcast interviews are done remotely, treat them as if you were in the studio sitting across from the interviewer. If you were sitting across from the interviewer, you would be engaged and fully present. This is exactly what you want to replicate.

Whatever you do, don't multitask. Even if you think you can quickly check an email or fire off a text, forget it. You can't. Drop whatever else is on your mind so that you're not distracted. If that means shutting off your computer or turning off notifications on your cell phone, do it.

Knowing how long the interview will last will help you pace yourself appropriately. Ask the producer or host how long the segment is before you begin recording. Keep track of the time as you interview. If you're going to use your cell phone to do this, make sure it's on silent and doesn't distract you from the conversation at hand.

DON'T ARGUE

As part of being concise and using the short amount of time you have on TV and podcasts wisely, move past any factual errors a reporter might inadvertently make. It's incredible how many times little bits of information, such as job titles, are wrong. Would you prefer your interviewer gets those minor details correct? Sure. However, is it a point worth correcting? No. With such tight time constraints, any seconds you use to correct errors are only taking away from the time you have to accomplish your mission and deliver your message.

Furthermore, your corrections make the interviewer look incompetent. You want the interviewer to be your ally, so do whatever you can to cultivate a friendly, positive, upbeat back-and-forth.

Your best tactic is to take preventative measures by

sending the reporter your digital press kit or even product samples ahead of time.

YOU'VE GOT THIS!

Television and podcast interviews are a fantastic opportunity to get your message out and build a strong reputation with a large or targeted audience. At first, these mediums might feel a little awkward, but with a little preparation and practice, you'll soon rattle off your core message and easily navigate all of the questions interviewers throw at you.

CHAPTER EIGHT

PRINT AND ONLINE INTERVIEWS

Print and online media are different beasts from broadcast mediums. The process of interviewing for these channels is somewhat different because you don't have to concern yourself with things like appearance, voice quality, energy levels, and the repetition of your core messages in sound-bite form. However, there are other things you *do* need to be aware of, which we will discuss in the pages to come.

MAXIMIZE YOUR PRINT AND ONLINE MEDIA HITS

Whether you're interviewing with a print or online

media channel, there are certain things you'll want to take into account and strategies you want to put in place. To a degree, your process will be the same, regardless of whether you are appearing in a print or digital outlet. Following are some concepts that apply equally to both mediums. Later on in this chapter, we'll look at some considerations specific to interviewing with online media channels.

ESTABLISH RAPPORT

The journalist you're interviewing with is there to do a job, just like you are. However, the best interviews often come in the course of natural conversation—or, at least, in the course of a conversation that feels natural. Also, this is someone you may want to pitch to again in the future. Interviews are a prime opportunity to make a human connection and solidify your relationship.

A good interviewer will often do the work of setting you at ease and establishing rapport. You should also feel free to contribute to this, or even do the work of establishing that easy back-and-forth when necessary. It's almost always possible to find some common ground. This can be as simple as using the information you gleaned from the pitching process and bringing up an article the journalist has written that you loved or found interesting.

The beauty of print and online interviews is that you are not as pressed for time as you will be in broadcast interview scenarios. While you want to respect the interviewer's time, taking a few minutes to create a connection and natural back-and-forth is well worth it, and will lead to a better article in the long run.

SET PARAMETERS

If there's something you absolutely don't want to discuss in an interview, such as a pending litigation or touchy business issue, be clear about it before the interview begins. Most journalists will respect your wishes. If, for some reason, they don't, just remind them that you're unwilling to comment when the topic comes up.

Along the same lines, you can attempt to guide the journalist if you feel it is necessary. You might say something like, "These are really the three main issues I'd like to discuss." This is a great way of setting yourself up to stay on-message. You are free to explicitly state that you would like to plug something. Journalists are well aware that this is the driving purpose behind interviews. You might say something like, "I'd really like to talk about my latest book," or, "I'd love the opportunity to tell your readers about the videos on my website."

Journalists understand that you're giving them a story, and you need to see some benefit for your time and effort, just as they do. But if you don't ask them to bring it up, they might not ask. This is why it's important to go into every interview—regardless of the media channel—knowing what you want to say and what you want to get out of it.

SPEAK CAREFULLY

In TV and podcasts, the words you choose are the words the audience hears. But in print and online media, the reporter might refashion your words. While you want to concentrate on repeating your message again and again for television and podcasts, print and online media requires that you focus on the clarity of your message so it isn't misinterpreted.

Rarely will a reporter intentionally try to twist your words. But, like a game of telephone, things are often lost in translation as it passes from you to the reporter to that reporter's transcription, and then to an editor and proofreader. Even slight wording changes can have a big impact on your message. The more to-the-point and clear you are, the less the chances are of this happening.

Be very precise, and make sure the interviewer understands what you're saying. If you get the impression something is lost in translation or a point isn't landing, offer to reexplain in a more straightforward manner. The journalist wants to get it right. It's up to you to help them do that.

BE THE STORY

On occasion, you may be asked to talk about a competitor. If that happens, steer the discussion back to you and your company. Never discuss a competitor in any way, shape, or form. Why give your press time and space to a rival? This is especially true online, as the reporter is likely to include a link to any other companies that might be mentioned. You are effectively driving traffic to your competitor.

Less intuitive is the fact that, unless the story is about companies using your product or service, it's best not to give away too much information about your customers. Reporters are always looking for the best angle to tell a story, which means, regardless of the story you pitched, the article is fluid until it's published. Sometimes, a story that started off being about you might morph into an article about your customers or the industry. To mitigate this risk, keep the story centered on you, your company, and your core message.

Cameron once did an interview about how he coached executives to create a positive company culture. During the course of the interview, he mentioned the name of one of his clients. The writer decided he wanted to interview that client. When the story ran, it was split about fifty-fifty between Cameron—who was intended to be the sole subject of the story when the interview began—and his client, who wasn't in the picture at all to start. By mentioning his client by name, Cameron inadvertently opened a door that was better left closed.

STAY ON YOUR TOES

The sense of urgency that accompanies on-air broadcasts isn't present in print and online interviews. When you're interviewed by a reporter for a print or online publication, they will likely record the conversation with a smartphone or take notes by hand. Sometimes they'll do both. Without cameras or microphones, the interview feels more casual, and there's a greater tendency to let your guard down.

The upside of this is that it's easier to get comfortable and relax, which can make for a great interview and enjoyable experience. The downside is it's easier to veer off message when you're relaxed. No matter how charming the reporter is or how relaxed you feel, remember: don't go off the record, with the exception of one specific scenario, which we'll get into shortly.

Going off of the record means whatever you discuss with the journalist is not eligible to be referenced in their story. However, for better or worse, nothing is *really* off the record when you talk to a reporter. A few years ago, Adrian did an interview with *Fast Company* about his company CanvasPop's integration with Instagram. The journalist was smart and reputable. The planned discussion came to an end, and the interview felt like it was over. Adrian and the reporter continued to talk, falling into what felt like a natural conversation, despite the fact that it was still being recorded. The reporter asked Adrian about his experience working with Kevin Systrom, the founder and CEO of Instagram. Adrian gave an honest, insightful answer.

The article was ultimately entitled, "An Insider's View on Instagram." Nothing discussed prior to Systrom was even referenced. Although Adrian's heart initially sank when he saw the article, it was ultimately still good for CanvasPop to be associated with Instagram in a top-tier publication. Still, it was not the article Adrian had intended, and it opened the door to a scenario that had the potential to go terribly wrong.

Adrian had his wits about him and didn't share any information about Instagram or Systrom that was off the record, but that's not always the case. It's easy to want to share nonpublic information or talk about something you have in the works when you're in the midst of a conversation with someone who appears genuinely interested in what you're talking about. Sometimes, a conversation with a journalist can start to feel a lot like a conversation with a friend. Always remember the journalist isn't your friend, at least in this context. This is a professional conversation, which will ultimately be shared with the world.

You should be okay with seeing anything you say—on or off the record—in print. If you don't want something to get out, don't share it. Period. There will be plenty of time to divulge this information in the future when you're ready to tell the world about your awesome new idea or product.

To be clear, it's not that journalists are out to get you or unethical. In fact, there are a lot of ethics involved in journalism, and the vast majority of reporters are very dedicated to operating within ethical standards. Still, there are plenty of ways in which you can find yourself addressing an off-the-record topic once you're back on the record. It's all part of the same conversation, and it's human nature to have a difficult time parsing these topics out.

In a worst-case scenario, a journalist can twist or

spin an on-the-record piece of information in such a way that you end up explicitly spilling the beans or implicitly confirming information. Reporters don't do this because they're jerks. They are doing their job, which is to gather information for readers. Ultimately, it's the audience and outlet they work for that journalists are accountable to.

PRO TIP: INTERVIEWING OVER EMAIL

Most journalists will have strong thoughts on interviewing over email, whether they're in favor of or against it. Some will view it as a great time-saver because they don't have to take notes or transcribe interviews. Others feel they lose out on an organic back-and-forth. Either way, there's no harm in asking. Just make sure the journalist knows you're flexible and willing to work with them in whatever way they prefer.

Answering interview questions over the email method allows you to take your time and thoughtfully articulate your response in a written format. It gives you maximum control over your interview.

When responding over email, make sure to include links or references to your site in your quotes so the publication links to you. Finally, be sure that you are aware of the reporter's deadline and—by all means—don't miss it!

FACT-CHECK

Very rarely in this day and age do you get the opportunity to fact-check an interview before it's published. Tight deadlines simply don't allow for it.

One way to get out in front of any accuracy issues is to send the writer a link to your press kit prior to the interview. In this, you'll want to include the core facts of your story and any relevant documentation. This saves the writer some time and effort and ensures that those facts will—or at least *should*—be correct when the story goes to press.

ONLINE MEDIA CONSIDERATIONS

Many companies place their emphasis on pitching to print publications because they are considered more prestigious in some circles. Print media is great, but they are also more selective because their space is limited.

There's another way to think of this, too. Yes, print is prestigious, but how many people are actually subscribing to print publications these days? As you are strategizing, think it through realistically. Go ahead and pitch to print sources but not at the cost of ignoring online outlets and the many benefits they have to offer.

Also, be aware that print publications like magazines often write articles three to four months before the article is printed (this is called "lead time"), which means that if you're pitching a holiday gift story for Christmas, you would have to pitch as early as August to make their deadline.

HUNGER FOR CONTENT

Online media has an insatiable appetite for content. Never before have we seen the demand for content in the volume we do right now. Newspapers and magazines are constrained by production costs and space. Delivering hard-copy publications also costs money, as does buying shelf space at brick-and-mortar venues. Given the cost of producing and marketing print publications, it's no wonder newspaper and magazine publishers are highly selective and only run enough content to fill a finite number of pages.

Of course, the internet isn't bound by these constraints. Material and delivery costs don't exist, so there's no need to kill stories for lack of space—which often happens with print. The amount of content an online media outlet can produce is unlimited. In fact, the more content a publication produces, and the more readers click on those stories, the more money the publication makes from advertisers.

Demand for online content is steady, enormous, and never-ending. Another huge bonus is that content lives online forever. Perhaps most valuable of all is the fact that readers have the ability to share articles with ease, which disseminates them to a broader, more expansive audience. You can use this to your benefit and fan the flames through your own media assets, helping spread the stories like wildfire in ways you never could in print.

BLOGGERS

Bloggers are the internet's equivalent of television or podcast hosts. These writers are less formal than their counterparts at more corporate websites and online publications. Generally, they have their own style and angle that separates them from traditional news sites. Just as you would prepare for a late-night talk show or satire program, you need to familiarize yourself with the blogger's style and personality. Who is their audience? What sort of questions can you expect from them? Take a look at their site before your interview to determine which of their stories garner the most engagement.

As always, you want to stay on message and provide links. Since they are generally a one-person operation, bloggers will usually happily accept any photos you provide to run alongside your story. Most bloggers have small budgets and won't have photographers on staff, which means providing images is up to you.

IMAGES FOR PRINT AND ONLINE PUBLICATIONS

Ideally, your published article will include images that visually appeal to the reader and draw them into your story. Cameron once did a newspaper interview about the state of employment. At the end of his conversation with the reporter, Cameron suggested an image of the CEO of his company standing at the front of a room full of empty office chairs. The goal of this image was to drive home the thirty openings Cameron was trying to fill at his company.

The reporter liked the idea and sent a photographer out to get the shot. When the story ran, it made the cover of the career section, with the photo occupying 75 percent of the page. The image was so powerful and impactful that it was the best way to tell the story and, arguably, more effective than the actual text. A single photograph captured the essence of the article in a way words couldn't.

In the course of your interview, you will want to discuss potential images. You can offer to send the reporter photos to supplement the story, or the publication may have their own photographer to take proprietary photos. Prepare for this conversation by brainstorming potential images ahead of time.

Don't pitch just any photo. You want to come up with an image that encapsulates the point you're trying to drive home to readers in as impactful a way as possible. As you can see from Cameron's experience, putting some effort into this process can pay off hugely. Before you sit down for the interview, think about how you might visually represent your story, and then take the initiative and pitch your idea to the writer at the end of your interview.

Some publications will prefer to source photos from your collection, while others will have a photographer on hand to send to you. If you are providing the images, make the process as easy as possible for the news outlet by having your own professionally taken photos easily accessible in your digital pressroom. The key phrase here is *professionally taken.*

PRO TIP: CREATE A DIGITAL PRESSROOM

Your pressroom doesn't have to be any more elaborate than a Dropbox folder reserved for the specific purpose of holding your professional images so that the media can easily access them.

Make your pressroom look professional by neatly organizing your photos in easy-to-find folders. Categorize your images in folders titled Product, Lifestyle, Logo, Headshots, and any other relevant categories.

Save your files in both web-resolution (72 DPI) and full-resolution images (10 megabytes or more). You can include low-res versions of your images in story pitches by embedding or linking (never attaching) to them. Let journalists know that you also have full-resolution images available for their use should they decide to run the story.

STOCK PHOTOGRAPHY

Not every media outlet will have the resources to send a photographer to your business. This doesn't mean no photos for you. Like any good PR rep, you will be armed with a series of professional shots to distribute at a moment's notice. When you receive a request for them, simply point the journalist to your digital pressroom.

In this context, "stock photography" refers to a collection of photos on hand for media usage. It's important that you never use stock photographs in the universal sense—you always want to have your own proprietary photos, rather than sourcing generic photos online. No matter how professional stock photos are, they are never a substitute for original images.

PRODUCT SHOTS

Product shots should be taken against a white background because it makes them easy for publications to use. Ensure that these photos feature only your product and don't include any unnecessary distractions.

If your product is an app or software, take high-resolution screenshots, and scrub out things like the name of the cell phone carrier, battery percentage, and any other distracting and unnecessary details that are present on your screen. You want readers to focus on the product, not the fact that you only have 2 percent battery left on your phone.

LIFESTYLE SHOTS

Lifestyle shots will demonstrate your product or service being actively used. For obvious reasons, lifestyle shots often feature people interacting with your product. The idea here is to bring your product to life and to create context around it. If you use people in your shots, make sure you obtain the necessary rights. This can be accomplished by having them sign a simple release form.

GET PERMISSION

Download a template photo release form at freeprbook.com/tools.

LOGOS

You should have your company logo available for journalists in two high-resolution formats: EPS (which works across the board) and JPEG or PNG. You will want to use a transparent background for your JPEG so that you don't end up with an unprofessional white block around your logo.

Some companies provide color variants for logos. If you choose to do this, make sure you name the file clearly so that reporters can easily find the color they need. Also, make sure you don't include any colors you don't actually want journalists to use—you'd be surprised how often this happens. In general, if you have a photo you don't want a journalist to use, don't include it in your pressroom.

HEADSHOTS

Your entire management team should have up-to-date professional headshots available. These photos should be taken by a professional photographer in a professional format, and they should all be consistent. Nothing says amateur more than a haphazard collection of leadership headshots in different styles, with different backgrounds.

As long as your headshots are professional and consistent, you can have some fun here. (Although you also want to have standard white-background headshots available for journalists.) Your headshots should reflect your brand. For example, Adrian has a headshot of him holding a cat. It was ridiculous, but it fit with the vibe of his company and was memorable.

WORKING WITH MEDIA PHOTOGRAPHERS

As we discussed in the previous chapter, when the media outlet you're working with handles photography, the goal is always to bring the photographer into your environment or an environment that's conducive to the message you want to convey. This is often very straightforward—for example, you will invite the photographer into your actual place of business. Or perhaps, after some consideration, you've decided that a quirky setting might best convey your message. For example, you bring the photographer to a ropes course that ties in with your company-culture story angle.

The more you can bring the media into your company, the more information they're able to acquire about it, and the more they can infuse that impression and those details into the story. A photo shoot under your jurisdiction allows reporters the chance to connect even more with your company. The more they're able to do this, the more vibrantly and specifically they can explain your business to their audience, through both words and images.

THE WALLS TELL A STORY

You've probably heard the expression, "The walls have ears." Guess what? Walls also have mouths. And those walls speak to the camera about the culture of your company and communicate a lot about your brand.

The Hootsuite offices in Vancouver are a fantastic example of how walls tell stories. One of their offices is aptly named the Winter Cabin. It has the feel of an actual chalet atop a ski hill, with old skis and snowshoes all around, a snowmobile, and stacked wood. It is decorated in Restoration Hardware furniture and feels incredibly cozy. They also have a Summer Cabin with its own distinctive features.

Obviously, not every company has the resources to get this intricate with their design and theme. However, it is possible to incorporate distinctive, homey touches in your office without the sort of money that Hootsuite spent on their cabin theme. Unique touches are great to show off to the media because they convey elements of your company's personality and vibe that words can't.

STAGING

As you think through media pictures, you want to look not just at the overarching story the photo tells but also at the details. It sounds simplistic, but many people forget about this. And it shows, once the photos run. Make sure that anyone who will appear in media photos has plenty of advance notice. Think of it like school picture day. Even employees should sign releases if possible.

The same goes for any inanimate objects appearing in photographs. Office windows should be spotless. Floors should be vacuumed; desks and communal space should be uncluttered. Company vehicles should be freshly washed and detailed, all the way down to having their tires polished.

All of this might sound a bit obsessive, but remember: these photos tell a story about you and your brand. While it's unlikely that readers will be consciously analyzing them, we all subconsciously form opinions based on small cues. That's what human beings are designed to do. Make sure your pictures send an irresistible message about your brand and the people behind it.

LEVERAGING YOUR MEDIA HITS

Now that you've done the work of earning valuable press hits, you want people to see them. Cameron once worked with a company that landed a story in the *Wall Street Journal*. As you can imagine, it was thrilling! Employees high-fived, celebrated, and congratulated one another on earning such a high-profile story in a premier business publication.

The only problem is that no one except for the employees ever saw the piece. The phone didn't ring. Revenue didn't increase. Literally, nothing happened.

It was a sobering but unforgettable reminder that press isn't like traditional marketing. Yes, media hits have a great potential to generate calls and business leads, but only if you leverage them. Landing stories in the media is only part of the work and purpose of coordinating your PR efforts. What you do after the story hits is just as vital.

THE RULE OF 27

The Rule of 27 holds that people need to see something nine times before they take action. Also, people only see one of every three things in front of them. If you do the math, this means that one person needs to be exposed to something twenty-seven times before taking action.

If the Rule of 27 is true—and, in our experience, it is—no matter where your articles appear, your potential customer needs more exposure than just a single read or view to take the action you want them to. This means it's up to you to push your press further and amplify its reach so that people see, hear, and read about your company again and again.

It's nothing short of critical to share good press on your company's LinkedIn, Facebook, Twitter, and other social media profiles. You want to ask your employees to share it on their social media pages, as well. And, of course, you want everything to link back to your website. This helps build SEO so that you climb to the top of Google searches.

When 1-800-GOT-JUNK? was on *Oprah*, the phone rang like crazy for a day. Then it was over. We weren't on *Oprah* anymore. The fact that Cameron has been able to tell the Oprah story over the course of the ensuing thirteen years is ultimately what has mattered the most. This is what leveraging is all about. Long after the initial thrill of an article or appearance has passed, you can still use it to your advantage through marketing, sales, and subsequent PR hits. The fact that Cameron can tell every journalist he speaks to that his company was on *Oprah* is more valuable than the business that came in because he was on the show.

Along with leveraging your press, you also want to leverage the relationships you build as a result. Adrian had to work hard to appear in *TechCrunch* for the first time. After that, it got easier and easier as he developed a rapport with the journalists who worked there.

Patience is key. As in any other area of life, it also takes time to build solid relationships with the media. Often, it also takes multiple avenues. After you interview with a journalist, interact with them on social media. Make them familiar with your name in an organic, likeable way. Just knowing a journalist won't guarantee you future press. You still have to have the story, and the journalist has to have an audience who wants to hear your story. However, relationships do help lubricate the process.

GETTING OTHERS TO LIKE AND SHARE YOUR STORIES

Even more than getting people to see your press hit, you want them to engage with it. When a story is published online, your goal is for as many people as possible to like and—even better—share it. This includes your team and your network of family, friends, and associates. Algorithms are becoming more sophisticated every day, and they can distinguish between passive and engaged viewers. An algorithm can determine whether or not someone actually read a story or just liked it in passing. Algorithms also account for the comments section; they track not only whether or not people leave comments, but also the length of and even the words used in those comments.

Your goal is to have people not only share your information, but also engage with it. One of the best ways to drive engagement is by engaging yourself. Spark a dialogue by contributing to discussions in the comments section. Make sure you reply to both positive and negative comments. Interacting with negative comments gives you the opportunity not only to potentially turn an opinion around, but also to demonstrate that you are listening and responsive to feedback.

This is good for measurables, and it's also good business. When you engage, it shows that your company doesn't just talk—it also *listens* and absorbs input from customers, clients, and the public. It shows you're invested in what's happening around you, and the people who are impacted. All the better if you can also get your founder or CEO on board to comment as well. This is a little thing that can go a long way and sends a strong message about your company's commitment and dedication.

Also, be sure to pin all positive articles to the top of your social media pages. This will get you more eyeballs and more engagement. When you post them, tag the journalist so that they get some promotion. This is an easy way to build your relationship with the press and keep those articles coming.

Make sure that all online media links back to your products and services. The initiative is on you to send reporters links to specific pages for inclusion. A few media outlets won't include links in their articles, but most will. In a case where a publication has a no-link policy, you can always provide a link in the comments section, in a nonpromotional way.

You want these links to take readers to specific landing pages, rather than your home page. Remember, the point of these stories is to bring in more business, so lead them directly to the "sale." Make it easy for them. Another benefit of getting links from media sources is that they create "link juice" to your site and enhance search engine optimization.

PRO TIP: DRIVE ENGAGEMENT

Maximize online media hits and engagement by using a paid advertising campaign on Facebook or other prominent social media sites to drive your audience to positive articles with prestigious media outlets. This type of advertising provides invaluable social proof and ensures that you will get more eyes on great press than simply linking to the article on your newsfeed.

YOU'VE GOT THIS!

Interviews with print and online publications can feel more informal and less pressurized than broadcast interviews. In some ways, they are. Precisely because of this, it's important to stay on your game. Connect with the reporter, but also make sure you stay on message, on track, and take the initiative necessary in terms of photos, links, and engagement to maximize the opportunity.

CHAPTER NINE

KEEP PEOPLE BUZZING

In the course of running DNA11, Adrian realized there was an untapped market in the photo-printing space. While DNA11 was a million-dollar-a-year business, it was still a lifestyle business. Adrian wanted to enter the much larger, multibillion-dollar-a-year photo-printing business. To his great benefit, Adrian already had the knowledge, ability, and equipment to print artwork, thanks to DNA11. So he launched CanvasPop, a large-format web-based printing company. Less than a decade later, CanvasPop is an eight-figure business.

DNA11 had instilled in Adrian the lesson that it

wasn't necessary to spend money for exposure. He followed this same philosophy with CanvasPop. Adrian made it his goal to get CanvasPop featured in the mother of all spaces: Times Square. Impossible, right? He did some digging and discovered that PRWeb was running a special. Anyone who paid $1,000 to run a press release with them would get their photo beamed onto Times Square for an additional $200.

Of course, this photo would only run for about fifteen seconds, but it was a start. Adrian cut a deal with PRWeb to buy one hundred of those slots at a discounted rate of $100 each. Of course, this isn't free, but $10,000 for advertising in Times Square is still a steal.

Adrian still thought he could do more. So, he went to various media publications and told them CanvasPop was going to do something no one had ever done before—offer the first hundred customers to their site the opportunity to have their picture displayed in Times Square for an additional cost of just $35. With this, Adrian gained a ton of press coverage and simultaneously covered a large portion of CanvasPop's costs to advertise.

The result? From day one, CanvasPop looked like a multimillion-dollar company, despite the fact that they were just a handful of guys from Ottawa. Thanks to some out-of-the-box thinking, CanvasPop's Times Square stunt led to them being featured on the *Today Show, Good Morning America,* and *TechCrunch.*

This guerrilla tactic drives home an important point. Generally, news is not only drab by nature, but it's also recurring. Audiences see, read, and hear many of the same news stories again and again. They crave anything out of the ordinary. So with a little thought, planning, and an honest assessment of your personality and company culture, you can hit it big in the media by thinking creatively about news stories and angles.

GET OUTSIDE OF THE BOX

On an average thirty-minute news broadcast, the first twenty-five or so minutes are devoted to what we might loosely call hard news. This follows the old axiom, "If it bleeds, it leads."

These lead stories are about the goings-on in the

city or, if it's national news, the country. Because so much of this content is negative and depressing, broadcasts like to finish on a lighter note. Sometimes that lighter note is a story about a kid overcoming a disease or hardship, sometimes it's a story about a Good Samaritan, sometimes it's about animals—a squirrel on tiny water skis or a friendship between a donkey and a goat. Other times, that feel-good story is about a company giving back to a community or organization. You can see where we're going.

The media needs inspirational tales. Especially in today's climate, these quirky or feel-good stories have the power to go viral. At some point, these stories spark a cultural zeitgeist, and the event becomes a touchstone that is embedded in pop culture. Just like that waterskiing squirrel.

If you're willing to be a little silly—assuming silliness suits the culture of your company—then, by all means, pitch a stunt for this slot of the news. However, if this type of thing isn't aligned with your brand personality, or if your culture is buttoned-down, don't try to pull it off. It will come off as inauthentic and have the opposite effect of what you're going for.

ATTACH YOURSELF TO A BRAND OR EVENT

Once upon a time, attaching yourself to a brand or event meant sponsoring something for charity and getting your photo taken with a giant check. That's old hat. Nobody gets excited about oversized checks these days, and a good media outlet isn't going to run that story.

We're not suggesting you shouldn't raise money for charity. What we *are* saying is don't do it for the photo op. It won't get you the exposure you're hoping for.

Cameron's blue-wig stunt raised money for charity, which is great. But it also attached his brand to the Vancouver Canucks. A Canadian company attaching itself to a hockey team is about as close to perfect alignment as you will ever find. The media loved the story because not only did it give them a chance to talk about charity, but it wrapped it up in a fun story about the passion and fervor of Vancouver fans.

Attention-grabbing publicity stunts are well suited for trade shows, which the media will already be covering. With the exception of a few larger annual conventions, trade shows are generally inside-baseball events that no one on the outside cares a fig about. In these instances, you have the opportunity to hook the media by flipping the script.

One of Cameron's companies did just that. Instead of hiring a local model to stand around in a bikini, they brought a few puppies from the SPCA to their booth each day. Talk about an easy sell! Who doesn't love puppies? It also highlighted the cause of homeless animals. Naturally, the media covered this—most audiences love those types of stories.

PRO TIP: USE AWARDS TO YOUR ADVANTAGE

Winning awards is a super simple way of both marketing and gaining credibility that most people don't think about. We've all seen the shiny logos at the bottom of websites—Designer of the Year Award, Best Customer Service Award, Top 50 Places to Work in California. The list goes on.

Even if you've never heard of the specific award before, seeing that a company has earned itself an award of any variety adds credibility and provides social proof. We call it halo branding. Those little review icons at the bottom of your page represent instant credibility.

This matters, whether you are looking to hire the best employees or stand out among your competitors. "Award-winning" is definitely an adjective you want to precede your company name.

There are thousands of awards out there. Be proactive about seeking them out and making yourself a contender. Once you win one, leverage it through social media, story pitches, and of course, by putting your very own shiny logo at the bottom of your web page.

GUERILLA MARKETING

Your goal is to have your company stand out from the rest. This means you need to get creative in telling your story. Guerilla marketing is one way to do this. This tactic consists of low-cost, innovative techniques that draw attention to your company. Buying a billboard is not guerilla marketing, because it costs a lot of money and anyone can do it. Adrian's Time Square stunt is.

Guerilla marketing doesn't have to involve a big spectacle or venue to be effective. At the Behance conference, which hosts the most creative people in the world, Adrian printed out mock fifty-dollar bills on canvas to distribute to attendees. With this, conference attendees—who also happened to be CanvasPop's target audience—received fifty dollars off of their printing order. Since Adrian used CanvasPop's machines to print the bills, the campaign cost very little. Attendees won by getting a big discount, and CanvasPop won because they earned new clients and made themselves memorable to their target audience.

Guerilla marketing is the perfect opportunity to have some fun and get creative. But first, let's look at a few more examples of unique and effective guerilla-marketing tactics to get your juices flowing.

Today, Airbnb is worth $25 billion. Back in 2008,

they were $20,000 in credit card debt. To save themselves from bankruptcy, the founders made the obvious choice: to launch their own line of cereal boxes. Yes, cereal boxes. During the 2008 election, Airbnb produced two boxes of cereal, one featuring Barack Obama (Obama O's), and the other featuring opponent John McCain (Captain McCain). They had the cereal box covers printed, hot-glued them onto boxes, then filled the boxes with Cheerios and Captain Crunch. Airbnb sold what basically amounted to an arts-and-crafts project for forty dollars a pop.

This stunt garnered Airbnb hundreds of articles and thousands of unique visitors, not to mention revenue. What's most interesting about this stunt is that cereal boxes have nothing to do with Airbnb's business. Yet, they still managed to create a big splash, draw attention to their brand, and get out of credit card debt in less than a day.

Although we encourage you to think outside of the box, 3M got a lot of attention for thinking *inside* of the box. They wanted to draw attention to a product that reinforces windows with a thin, clear piece of glass that prevents windows from shattering. 3M decided to place one of their shields on a glass box filled with cash. They placed the glass box on a busy street in Vancouver and challenged passersby to smash the glass. Anyone who was successful could keep the money.

The only party that ended up making any money off of the event was 3M. No one could smash the box, and 3M got a ton of attention, which translated into millions of dollars in sales. Not only was this campaign successful, but 3M also found a very clever way of showing people how their product worked that was far more effective and stickier than a run-of-the-mill advertising campaign.

Tinder had an incredible strategy for courting (excuse the pun) the Australian press. Director of marketing and employee number six, Josh Metz, shares the guerilla tactic the burgeoning company used to grab the attention of the press. When they were still an unknown entity in Australia, Tinder hired gorgeous models to go into the office of target publications, walk directly up to a specific journalist, and hand him or her a folded-up note that read, "This is not my number, but find me on Tinder." The model would then give the journalist a kiss on the cheek, turn around, and walk out.

As soon as they left the building, the models texted Josh to let him know they had accomplished their mission. Josh immediately followed up with an email that said, "Hey, I hope you enjoyed Daphne's visit. Here's a little bit more about Tinder since you're probably wondering what it is." Josh would then dangle another carrot by explaining the app was already taking off in the United States. This matters in a place like Australia, which often follows trends that start in larger markets such as America.

Journalists ate it up. Many of them booked time to speak with Tinder's founders, and the company quickly earned nationwide press. Their Australian user rate started to go through the roof after that point. None of this is surprising—not only did Tinder come up with a super creative idea, but it was also one that was designed to stick.

Finally, let's take a look at the Dollar Shave Club, which relied on social media to get their brand out there. They spent about $4,500 to make a video that went viral and ultimately generated more than one hundred million views on YouTube, $3.5 million in revenue that year alone, and single-handedly put the company on the map. Dollar Shave Club is now a billion-dollar company and, to this day, they still have the video on their website.

The beauty of the Dollar Shave Club video is that it didn't include any fancy bells and whistles. It relied on one simple thing we can all appreciate and relate to: humor. That's it. Simple, but extremely effective.

Notice that all of these campaigns are inexpensive and attainable. Although Airbnb, Tinder, and Dollar Shave Club are huge companies now, they were not at the time when they launched these campaigns. 3M was already a gigantic corporation, but even they didn't rely on money to get the job done—it was creativity and cleverness that made their campaign so successful.

IF YOU'RE GOING TO DO IT, DO IT RIGHT

Unfortunately, guerilla marketing has had its fair share of epic fails, too. People like to say that all press is good press, but the following examples prove otherwise.

In 1986, United Way staged what was perhaps the worst guerilla-marketing stunt ever when they launched 1.5 million balloons into the air over downtown Cleveland. What a beautiful display it must have been, right? Well, yes. At least for a few minutes. Unfortunately, the event organizers failed to think the stunt the whole way through. They didn't consider the weather, potential air-traffic delays and interruptions, or the waste that would result from this volume of popped balloons.

Disaster ensued. An incoming storm pushed the balloons back down toward the city. A Coast Guard helicopter could not make its way through the cloud of balloons to rescue two passengers from an overturned boat. Once the helicopter finally made its way to the area where the victims were drowning, they couldn't differentiate the balloons that now covered the surface of the water from the victims' heads. Two people drowned as a result. A horse was so spooked that it seriously injured itself, and the owner sued United Way to the tune of $100,000. This was in addition to the millions of dollars in lawsuits. It took the city of Cleveland weeks to clean up the mess the balloons had created.

The shooting video game *Call of Duty* staged a guerilla-marketing stunt that involved setting up a fake news account and tweeting about a fake terrorist attack in Singapore. For obvious reasons, people were not amused by this very ill-conceived idea. *Call of Duty* completely failed to consider the current high-alert climate and people's sensitivity to terrorism. Don't make this mistake.

These are just a couple of many stunning examples of guerilla marketing gone wrong. Not all failures are as epic as these two, but you want to avoid a failure of any level in your own practice.

When you are planning a guerrilla-marketing stunt, carefully think it through from beginning to end. Have a few people weigh in on potential outcomes to incorporate different vantage points that you might miss. Have a clear understanding of what you want to achieve through the stunt. What is your best-case scenario? Does the stunt align with your brand in such a way that it will capture the attention of your potential customer base? If not, why do it?

You want to spend even more time thinking through your worst-case scenario. Is what you're doing illegal? Will anyone or anything be hurt? Is there any risk at all that the stunt could ultimately negatively impact your brand? If the answer to any of these questions is yes, how can you alter or tweak your plan to avoid the negative elements? *Can* they be avoided? If not, it's time to move on to plan B. Any risk is not worth it.

Finally, don't be afraid to learn from others. There are literally hundreds of websites out there with guerilla-marketing tactics that have worked (or not worked) for other companies. Feel free to use them for inspiration, and to identify where things might go wrong so that you can prevent a PR disaster from ever happening in the first place.

YOU GOT THIS!

Guerilla and stunt marketing afford you the opportunity to get creative and do something out of the ordinary that will catch people off guard. There are few things as gratifying as watching a stunt pay off huge. However, sometimes people get carried away with a grand plan and fail to think it through or believe the risks are worth it. Don't let yourself fall into that category. The sky is the limit when it comes to guerilla marketing, but you want to make sure you tether that plan in reality.

CONCLUSION

Now that you have all the tools and strategies you need to bring your PR program in-house, the only thing left is to get started.

If you think back to the very beginning of this book, you might remember that Cameron and Adrian had two different strategies to building their PR team at their respective companies. At 1-800-GOT-JUNK?, Cameron hired a team of people to take on the company's PR efforts. At DNA11, Adrian took on the PR role himself. What is the difference, and how should you know how you should structure the PR team in your own company?

SIZE DOES MATTER

The critical difference between Cameron and Adrian's situations was that Cameron was walking into an established company that already had revenue and, thus, a larger budget to dedicate to PR. After all, they were already paying $5,000 per month to outsource their PR.

Adrian was at the helm of a start-up business that was not yet profitable. For the simple reason of cost savings, it made more sense for Adrian to take on the company's PR efforts himself.

We can't give you a cut-and-dry number to help you understand whether it's time for you to bring on an in-house PR person. However, if you are in a scenario similar to Cameron's, where you are outsourcing a significant amount of money to a PR firm on a regular basis, it's time to consider spending that money on your own dedicated in-house PR representative.

As you begin to consider whether or not it's time for you to bring someone in-house, remember this: it is always powerful to have a CEO's name appear on an email to journalists. Of course, this is the person the journalist is going to have the most interest in communicating with when it comes time to interview. However, this doesn't mean that the CEO should be building media-outreach lists or sending follow-up pitch emails. Clearly, that's not the best use of any CEO's time. So, while company leaders may want to continue dipping their toe into their PR machine, it doesn't mean that they should be running the day-to-day minutiae of it after the point where it stops making sense in terms of both time and money.

MAKING THE FIRST STEP

Creating your in-house PR team means it's time to cut the cord with your PR firm. No matter how much money cutting your agency out will save you, it can still feel like jumping into an unknown void. This is particularly true for businesses that have relied on an outside PR firm for years. Pulling the trigger requires a leap of faith.

We've seen so many companies come up against this fear. But invariably, within just the first couple of weeks, they realize it's one of the best decisions they've ever made. By following the strategy we've outlined in this book, your own PR representative can be up and running in just a few weeks. In fact, they can even begin the process of researching media outlets and journalists and creating story angles while your current PR firm is still on retainer. This means that as soon as you cancel your contract with the agency, you can immediately get to work on your own PR efforts with no lag time whatsoever.

When Cameron first started doing his company's PR work, he would put in less than an hour a day on average. Even with this minimal amount of time, he got good results. Cameron realized that if he could do it and get results in less than five hours a week, he could teach others how to do it and get even more press attention.

Tyler was Cameron's first PR hire. Tyler already worked in the company's sales department. He had no experience whatsoever in the media space. What Tyler *did* have was an intimate understanding of both the company and the industry. He was thoroughly indoctrinated in the company culture. As Cameron suspected, Tyler was a great ambassador for the company because he believed in it, was loyal to it, and was part of it.

Within a couple of days, and with just a little

training, Tyler generated the same type of results Cameron was getting.

Chances are, you have a Tyler in your company as well—someone who knows your industry and the product; is a good, personable communicator; and has a history of selling. As we've discussed, selling strategies are extremely helpful in PR because both functions require persistence, relationship-building, and understanding how to present a product, service, or company in the best, most compelling light. If you tap that person for PR, they can be off and running in almost no time, providing you better PR than anyone on the outside could ever hope to.

FINDING SUCCESS

It's a lot easier to get free PR than most people think. But it's also important to understand what success looks like. It probably won't appear as a stampede of new customers beating down your door or your inbox and your Twitter feed exploding. Each new media story is a building block that will slowly generate more media stories for you and your company. You want to leverage each and every one of these blocks.

A successful free PR campaign will build the credibility of your company by generating third-party social proof. This idea isn't novel. In fact, it's what advertising did once upon a time, before audiences realized that companies could say anything they wanted to about themselves because they were paying through the nose for it.

PR generates momentum, which keeps accelerating over time. As you collect more and more media stories, your marketing team can repurpose them to align with their own strategies, and your human resources team can repackage them to promote a stronger company culture.

The stories you tell in the media have limited value. The lasting value is in what you do with those stories, how you share them, and how you leverage them to your advantage. When you do all of these things, PR becomes one of the most powerful tools in your entire arsenal.

ACKNOWLEDGMENTS

CAMERON WOULD LIKE TO THANK:

College Pro Painters, where I learned the art of Free PR.

1-800-GOT-JUNK?, where I perfected the art of Free PR and built out the most kick-ass team of experts ever.

ADRIAN WOULD LIKE TO THANK:

Andrea Renaud, my life partner and best friend who put up with me while I worked on this book and provided me with endless hours of support and encouragement.

Dan Martell, for his valuable advice and energetic personality.

Harley Finkelstein, for his wisdom, advice, and friendship when I needed it the most.

Seth Godin, for inspiring me, teaching me through his books, and encouraging me to be "remarkable."

Matt Whitteker, a true friend, sounding board, and beacon of light.

Peter Shankman, for coaching me and inspiring me to take the first step toward coauthoring this book.

Zach Obront and Tucker Max, for making this book possible through their amazing company Scribe Media.

Nikki Van Noy, our amazing writer who spent countless hours with me on the phone helping to take my words, thoughts, and ideas to craft this book.

Cameron Herold, for allowing me to be part of this book and for being a coach, mentor, and friend for more than a decade.

ABOUT THE AUTHORS

CAMERON HEROLD

Cameron Herold is an international speaker and author of *Meetings Suck* and the best-selling book *Double Double: How to Double Your Revenue and Profit in 3 Years or Less*, which is currently in its seventh printing. He is also the coauthor of *Miracle Mornings for Executives* and *Vivid Vision*.

Cameron is the mastermind behind hundreds of companies' exponential growth and has built a dynamic consultancy, including his time as COO of 1-800-GOT-JUNK?. His current clients include everyone from a Big 4 wireless carrier to a monarchy. He is the founder of COO Alliance, which helps COOs become better leaders.

Cameron's work has helped companies get noticed in the Associated Press, *Bloomberg*, *USA Today*, the *New York Times*, *Wall Street Journal*, *Fast Company*, and *Fortune*, as well as such television shows as the *Oprah Winfrey Show*, *The Big Idea with Donny Deutsch*, and *Dr. Phil*.

ADRIAN SALAMUNOVIC

Adrian Salamunovic is the cofounder of DNA11 and CanvasPop, which he bootstrapped to eight-figure sales. He is also a start-up advisor, investor, and PR expert who is passionate about helping entrepreneurs amplify their companies. Adrian has strategized the launch and continued success of many businesses, helping both his own and his clients' companies generate hundreds of millions of free media impressions.

Adrian has attained massive exposure to launch brands into mainstream success. His companies have been featured in the *New York Times*, *Wall Street Journal*, *Today Show*, *Good Morning America*, *The Big Idea with Donny Deutsch*, CNN, MSNBC, *TechCrunch*, Mashable, *Fast Company*, *Forbes*, The Verge, and *WIRED*. Adrian even had an episode of *CSI: NY* written around one of his products.

Made in the USA
Monee, IL
28 July 2020